There Must Be A Reason
... to Believe the Bible

Maureen Lang

There Must Be A Reason

ISBN Print: 978-1-943210-36-7

Ebook: 978-1-943210-37-4

Copyright © 2023 by Maureen Lang

All rights reserved.

No part of this book may be reproduced in any form or by any electronic or mechanical means, including information storage and retrieval systems, without written permission from the author, except for the fair use of credited brief quotations or in a book review.

Scripture quotations from the ESV® Bible (The Holy Bible, English Standard Version®), © 2001 by Crossway, a publishing ministry of Good News Publishers. Used by permission. All rights reserved. The ESV text may not be quoted in any publication made available to the public by a Creative Commons license. The ESV may not be translated in whole or in part into any other language.

Scripture quotations marked NLT are taken from the Holy Bible, New Living Translation, © 1996, 2004, 2015 by Tyndale House Foundation. Used by permission of Tyndale House Publishers, Inc., Carol Stream, IL 60188. All rights reserved.

Scripture quotations marked CSB®, are taken from the Christian Standard Bible®, Copyright © 2016 by Holman Bible Publishers. Used by permission. Christian Standard Bible®, and CSB® is a federally registered trademark of Holman Bible Publishers.

Scripture taken from the Holy Bible, NEW INTERNATIONAL VERSION® Copyright © 1973, 1978, 1984, 2011 by Biblica, Inc.® Used by permission. All rights reserved worldwide.

Scripture quotations marked KJV are taken from the King James Version, which is in the public domain in the U.S..

References and paraphrases from *I Don't Have Enough Faith to Be an Atheist* by Norman L. Geisler and Frank Turek, © 2004, pp. 105-106. Used by permission of Crossway, a publishing ministry of Good News Publishers, Wheaton, IL 60187, www.crossway.org.

The websites and authors quoted are not endorsements of this book. They are quoted as resources for readers to explore.

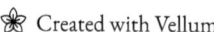 Created with Vellum

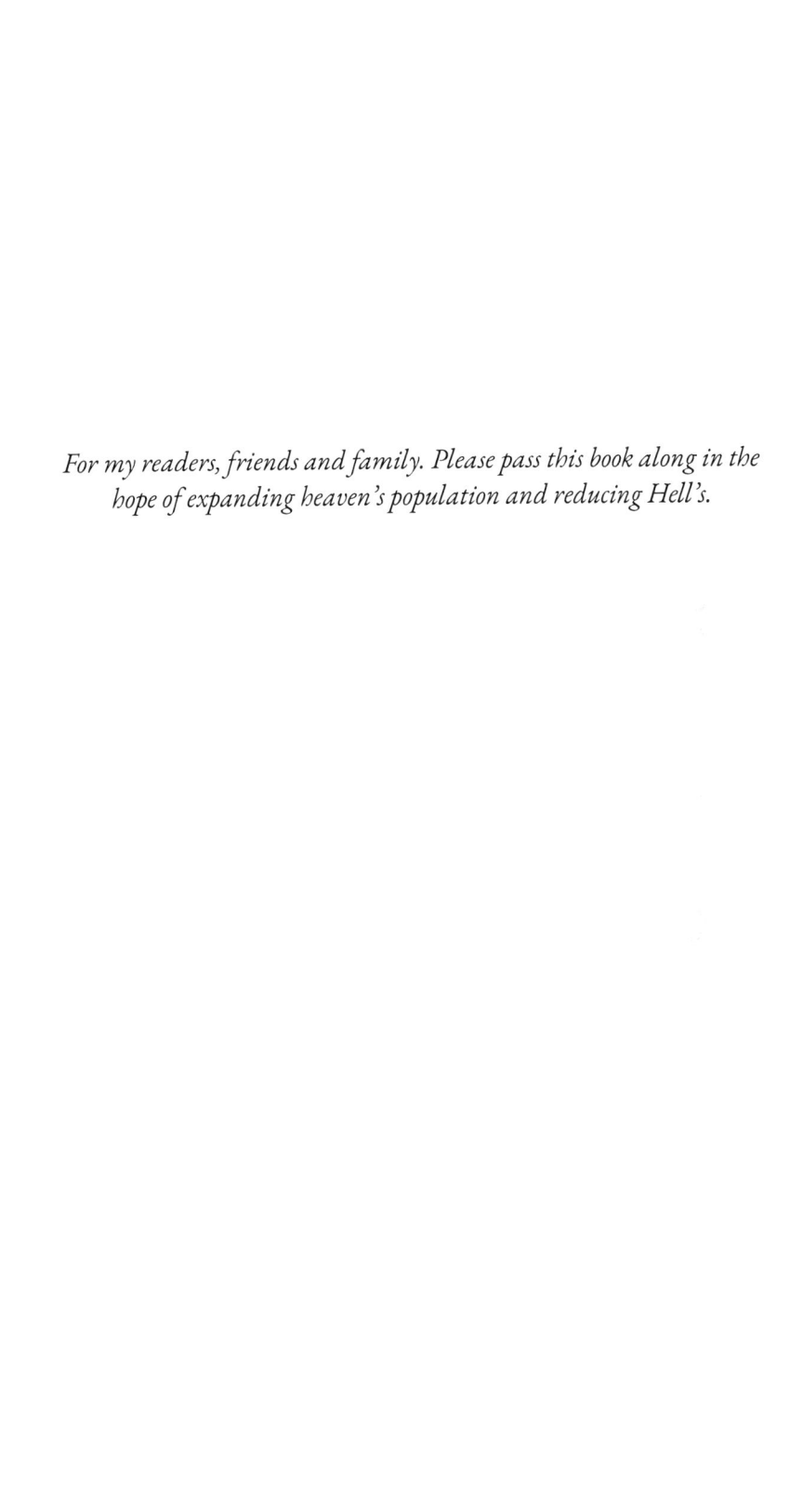

For my readers, friends and family. Please pass this book along in the hope of expanding heaven's population and reducing Hell's.

Contents

Preface	vii
1. Archeological & Historical Evidence	1
2. Science	20
3. Wisdom and the Human Experience	64
4. Prophecy	79
5. Personal Testimony & the Spiritual Realm	128
Afterword	153
Acknowledgments	157
Also by Maureen Lang	159
About the Author	161
Notes on Why You Believe	163

Preface

At the risk of having some readers discount anything written after this Preface, I admit I am not a scholar. But then, this book is largely aimed at those who either know me personally or are familiar with my other books, so you already know this. I claim my passion for research as my one and only credential.

I've used many different sources, books as well as online scholars, pastors, or other Believers. I looked at competing beliefs and opinions, to see if I could be persuaded away from some of the claims I'm presenting. And although I used my old habit of looking for more than one source to verify major claims, I didn't use footnotes as that, to me, would too closely mimic a more scholarly presentation. Finally, I expect varying reactions to my research or even my sources, since I've learned scholars and perhaps people in general can disagree with just about anything. That's why I implore some of my more sensitive readers to keep handy the friendly phrase "agree to disagree." This book is a presentation of the reasons I hold the Bible as the Word of God. I wrote this because each of us should know *why* we believe whatever we believe.

The process of putting my reasons into writing has certainly been a blessing, as I'd originally hoped. I learned new things, confirmed old things, my faith grew, and my concern for others who are missing the blessing of faith became more apparent. This project has encouraged me, so my prayer is it will do the same for readers.

But really, why write this?

Over the years, my husband, Neil, and I have had numerous discussions about faith. Some time ago we compiled a brief list of categories that remind us of the foundation of our faith in the Bible. If we believe this Book is one of two ways the Creator of the Universe communicated to us (the other being nature) it must be worth either challenging or accepting. In other words, the Bible shouldn't be ignored.

So why do we believe the Bible is the Word of God? Here are the categories that, for us anyway, provide the most compelling reasons:

- **History (archeological support)**
- **Science**
- **Wisdom (Timeless and universal knowledge of the human experience)**
- **Prophecy**
- **Testimonies as a result of faith in the Bible and proof of a spiritual realm**

A note on other religious books

Obviously there are other books considered holy by huge groups of people. However, the point of this brief, easy-to-read text is to clearly present reasons for my faith, not to attack others.

That said, I will spend a few pages on other major religions that contradict the Bible. Since two opposing views can't both be true, one must be false. Religions like Islam don't recognize Christ as God even though He said He was God (John 8:58, Revelation 1:8, among others), Mormons don't recognize the trinity and they both, along with other religions, believe the Bible has been corrupted. Islam does not teach the resurrection. Buddhists don't believe in a personal God. Hindus believe in many gods and, along with Buddhists and Falun Gong followers, believe in reincarnation. The Bible says there is One God eternally existing in three persons, Father, Son and Holy Spirit, and that we "are appointed once to die, then the judgment." (Hebrews 9:27) So, multiple gods and reincarnation oppose what the Bible says. Other faiths do not believe that faith in Christ alone is enough for salvation, as the Bible states. In John 14:6, as one example, Jesus said He is "the" way, not "a" way to heaven.

About Reincarnation

Reincarnation is an interesting idea as ideas go: karma coming around from life to life to reward or repay us for what we do. But why, if mankind has been reincarnated over and over since the beginning of human life, aren't we improving despite all the many chances through history to get life right? You might say we're getting worse. Is it because those who do finally live with kindness and virtue don't come back at all, which seems to be the goal? To reach the non-existent existence of nirvana? How does that improve the world?

My second question is related to the first. If each body we temporarily inhabit lives a life of good or evil, and the subsequent life is either rewarded or punished—we're blamed or rewarded for something our current body didn't do—then how do we repeat the good until it's good enough, or avoid the bad altogether? I guess karmic amnesia explains why we don't learn from past mistakes, and perhaps why the world isn't getting any better. But what is the purpose of this endless cycle if we can't learn from the many past lives we've endured?

A third question is if someone does live a good life and is rewarded in the next by money, power, or both, then why are so many people in power so corrupt? Wouldn't they be enjoying the rewards of goodness, only to spend that reward on evil?

But what about extraordinary accounts from those who remember what seem to be past lives? These experiences undoubtedly prove a spiritual realm. However, while such information about the past can be 100% correct, I believe it is deceptive evidence. What better way to distract us from the truth of Christ than convince us reincarnation is true? Demonic spirits are witnesses to the past and could be convincing for reincarnation—or psychics, too. In addition, predictions of the future may be remarkable based on thousands of years of observing human behavior, but only God knows the future with 100% accuracy.

The bottom line for reincarnation is to do good in your present life. This makes reincarnation like all other religions which require good works to find eternal peace. But how is it possible to be aware of peace if there is no sense of self in the eternal state? This, to me, is the opposite of Biblical teaching that God made each of us unique yet in His image, Who wants to spend eternity in fellowship. The God of the Bible loves us individually for who we are, body and soul, and when we do something wrong, we're offered forgiveness, not an endless but forgotten cycle in the hopes of working hard enough to finally end that cycle.

About Islam

Eyewitnesses to Muhammed's life never saw any miracles because even though he was challenged to perform such things, he never took up that challenge. He didn't claim to be God, he said he was a prophet. In the book *I Don't Have Enough Faith To Be An Atheist*, authors Geisler and Turek explain that miracles attributed to Muhammed were told by Muslims who lived 100 to 200 years after Muhammed. They wanted to prove Muhammed was a prophet, and so stories were gathered in the Hadith, a book that was compiled during the 8th and 9th centuries. Muhammed lived during the late 6th and early 7th centuries.

In fact, Muhammed didn't have a groundswell of support during or even just after his death. Near the end of his life, after his military campaigns were beginning to spread, he did start attracting more followers. This may partly have been because he raided Meccan caravans and divided the booty with his followers (people were already going to Mecca on religious pilgrimages well before Muhammed to worship various deities).

The growth of Islam differs with Christianity in many ways. One difference is that Christianity was a peaceful movement with many martyrs willingly giving up their lives because of a Messiah who spread God's love even though He threatened the status quo. Muhammed, on the other hand, spread Islam largely by military force. He seized Mecca during his lifetime, but after Muhammed's death his followers went on to conquer the Holy Land, then the rest of the Middle East, the Near East and Northern then Eastern Africa, Spain, and parts of Asia. Wherever Muslims conquered, they forced the losing side to give up their own faith and convert to Islam, or if they refused, to pay a tax to continue practicing their faith, become a slave, or be executed. It may have been practical to join the Muslims if you didn't want to leave your homeland or lose your life, but not necessarily a spiritual decision.

So . . . in the beginning of Christianity, you might have to give up your life because of somebody else's sword, but to spread the Islamic faith you might have to use your sword on somebody else. Even today, those who hold traditional Islamic beliefs approve the death sentence for apostates (those who leave their faith for another one, or no longer practice Islam).

Were you taught the Crusades happened so Europeans could convert Moors and "savages" to Christianity? First of all, in defense of early Islamic society, in some ways it was far less "savage" than early European society! A thousand years after the birth of Christianity, European campaigns went to the Middle East at the behest of Pope Urban II to help regain territory the Muslims had conquered. These military campaigns were an effort to regain territory, not to spread Christianity by force.

There are, of course, many instances in history where Christianity has been corrupted for power or even used for just pure evil. But the true Gospel has never had a part in any of that because Jesus renounced violence. Even Pilate recognized Jesus was being unfairly accused after Jesus said His kingdom wasn't of this world. Pilate declared Him innocent of all charges and washed his hands of the matter. Jesus also said to turn the other cheek when someone wrongs you. He is the Prince of peace and gave His life so we could have fellowship with God.

A note about Old Testament violence. As I readily claim, Jesus is God. God commanded not just the conquest of certain dangerously pagan societies, but the annihilation of everyone in such a society. Does that equate Jesus with the terrorists of today, who wish to annihilate those they consider infidels? No. God, the creator of all life, is in charge of life. At one time in history He was molding the Jewish nation to bring forth the Messiah to save all mankind. Not only did He protect it from especially brutal enemies, He wanted His people to be faithful to Him. Yet they kept wandering and being influenced by certain pagans. In order to wipe out not only especially evil enemies but also powerfully sinful influences, God ordered the annihilation of certain people groups. These were specific in scope and for that era only, and not condoned on a wide scale. All such acts ended with the coming of Christ, because God's mission to bring a Messiah through the line of David was fulfilled.

Being a Christian means trusting that Jesus really is God and Savior, trusting Him with your life and eternity, because of trust in the Bible's authority. As the saying goes, Christianity is a relationship with God, not a religion. Christians don't have to work for God's acceptance the way other religions demand, and you don't have to worry if you'll make it to heaven. Jesus did what we couldn't do by living a perfect life and freely lending us that perfection for acceptance by a perfect and holy God. There's no walking on a tightrope to see which way you'll fall, heaven or hell, or being reincarnated again and again until you work hard enough to "get it right." You have the assurance of heaven because the Bible tells us Jesus' death on the cross is enough, if you trust Him.

We may want to "do good" just because that's what'll happen when God's Holy Spirit takes up residence in our soul. Good works are an indicator of real faith, because His Spirit lives within us and reminds us one day we'll hear God Himself say "Well done, my good and faithful servant" for those things we wanted to do out of love and gratitude. But the truth is Jesus did what needed to be done to solve the problem of letting sinful beings spend eternity with a holy, holy, holy, God.

Christ and other religions

As J. Warner Wallace says (he's one of my favorite online teachers, you'll read more about him later), religions such as Islam, Baha'i, Krishna, Ahmadiyya (an offshoot of Islam), New Age and others either *modified* their beliefs to mimic Christianity, or *merged* Jesus into their beliefs, or at least *mention* Him as someone special. Buddhism says Jesus lived a self-sacrificial life, was a wise teacher, a Bodhisattva who delayed his journey to Nirvana out of compassion for others who suffer. Islamists call Jesus a prophet worthy of reverence.

While these and other religions have accommodated Christ in some way, Christianity has not changed to accommodate their central figures.

Man has been looking for certain attributes in a savior or god for as long as there has been human history. This search is part of the human experience. Many key religious figures fulfilled some of the ancient myths or expectations for a Deity, but only Jesus fulfills them all. From being a selfless sacrifice for flawed humanity to being our judge, from fulfilling prophecy to being a benevolent, personal God, someone immortal, an intercessor, a teacher on how to respond to God's call, and more. J. Warner Wallace compiled an extensive list of attributes other gods have sought to provide, but only Jesus meets them all. To investigate further I recommend his website, coldcasechristianity.com.

Another question skeptics often ask: if God created everything, who created God?

That answer must be found before the beginning of everything we know—in other words, before time began. This is how the Bible describes creation, as you'll see in the Science section.

No matter how you answer the question of creation, as a Believer, an atheist, or somewhere in between, it comes down to something eternal. Either there was an *impersonal*, uncaused first cause (an eternal universe/s with endless possibilities for an accident to somehow spark life out of nothing) or a *personal* first cause (God). Could some kind of multiverse or other scientific condition trace back to who caused the multiverse? But who caused whatever first cause you can imagine? It must go back eternally, which makes me think an eternal God who created everything out of nothing (including time as a measuring stick) makes more sense than an accident of nature creating something out of nothing. As Stephen Meyer says, there is no example in history in which information (like a human mind/DNA, etc.) came from anything other than intelligence, i.e. a design*er*/mind.

Is believing in the mind of God really such a fantastic leap, instead of believing the design and complexities of creation came out of nothing? As the aforementioned book title sums it: *I don't have enough faith to be an atheist.*

I include this thought because, over the years, I've met people who have developed their own religion. They're attracted to certain elements of various philosophies and sew those pieces together to create their own, tailor-made, personal answer to the God-shaped hole we're all born with. I marvel at the self-confidence this must take, for someone to ask the questions we all ask at one point: *Why is mankind here? Why am I here? What is the meaning of life?* and answer with: I don't need any other authority except myself. I'll use my own, unique wisdom to make up my own truth. After all, these days it's common to say "You're entitled to your truth, I'm entitled to mine."

Except, as already noted, if two opposing views contradict, then only one view can be true. It's reasonable to say you can't call various truths, truth, if they don't agree, right? In other words, how does a person holding truth as what "feels right" to be a universal truth? Because if truth is really true, it must be universal. We may have varying experiences and opinions, (some of us have harder or easier lives than others) but those questions come out of overarching truths that mean the same for all of us:

- We exist.
- The natural world is so beautiful and so fine-tuned it points to a created universe because it had a beginning out of nothing. Because of its beauty and variety, it seems the Creator wants us to enjoy creation. That suggests a personal, not distant or "hands-off" creator.
- None of us are perfect; sooner or later we hurt others or ourselves.
- When we hurt others or ourselves, we need to be forgiven to feel okay about ourselves again, because of our conscience.
- Who is the authority to offer forgiveness? Ourselves? The person we offended? What if that's not possible, or not enough to ease our guilt? Perhaps we need a savior offering forgiveness outside ourselves.
- It's easier to love others and ourselves better if we know we're already loved. When we're loved we can offer and receive forgiveness more easily. The personal Creator God of the Bible proves His love by the life, sacrificial death and resurrection, of Jesus Christ as reported in the Bible.

Mostly what I want to say about those who make up their own religion, is that the Bible offers more authority than any other holy document. Jesus Himself said He is the truth. This book explores why I believe *the* truth is found in the Bible.

The Bible is one of the most scrutinized, investigated and attacked books in history. I don't think it's an exaggeration to say Christianity, via the Bible, has been more influential in more regions of the world than any other document ever written. This one Book has had a universal influence on everything that sets humans apart from animals, including worship, art, architecture, literature, science, education and music. So even if I didn't hold the Bible as Holy Scripture, I would want to investigate its claims simply because it has impacted more people throughout the world, throughout history, than any other manuscript.

One final word in this section I should probably call "miscellaneous." There may be things written in this book that don't mesh with opinions, beliefs or doctrine of others, including Christians who love God just as much as I do.

First, it is not and never would be my intention to offend anyone, even though if you know me, I sometimes let — *passion* — touch some discussions. Offense may be the unintended result. For that, I sincerely apologize, particularly if I've repeated the scenario here.

Second, most importantly, is that the differences in doctrine I may have with other Christians are not likely to be a "big one"—in other words, we likely mesh with the core beliefs that Jesus Christ is God, He died on the cross and was resurrected, He is the only way to Heaven because His blood covers our shortcomings compared to a holy God, and the Bible, confirmed by creation, is the inerrant Word of God. The Bible and nature are love letters, so to speak—telling us He's there, He's personal, and He loves us. All we need to do is ask Him into our life and let Him guide us with the help of the Bible to navigate the gift of life.

For those readers who don't consider themselves Christians, I'm grateful you're giving me a chance to share these thoughts and beliefs. Feel free to read this in whole or only the parts that interest you most. It's incredibly generous of you to explore this in part or in whole! So, thank you from the get-go.

And now, let's go!

Archeological & Historical Evidence

Like science, as we'll address in the next segment, archeological progress has tended to go one way: the more we discover, the more archeology supports the Bible as remarkably accurate. And if the history and science are so incredibly right, why wouldn't the rest of it be right as well?

Biblical archeology took off in the 1800s, with British and American teams exploring many ancient sites. We can discuss another day about the manner in which these archeological digs were authorized and carried out, and we'd likely agree in many instances. Because of their work and work still being done today, the Bible has been proven again and again to be an accurate record of human history. According to Josh McDowell's book *Evidence That Demands a Verdict*, archeology cannot absolutely prove whether God exists, but it's come a long way to verify the trustworthiness of the text God provided for us.

A few highlights

In his comprehensive book just mentioned, Josh McDowell begins his segment on archeology with the Ebla Tablets. Ebla was an ancient city mentioned in ancient manuscripts, but until this archeological find in Syria, no one knew where such a city was or if, in fact, it even existed. Then around the late 1960s Italian archeologists started digging in a spot already of interest because of certain noticeable mounds. It wasn't until the mid-1970s that they hit the jackpot: a major regional center from the Bronze Age, including a palace and, most importantly, a library.

Here's the basics for this important discovery. Moses, who lived about 1400 BC, wrote the first five books of the Old Testament (the Pentateuch). Critics of the Bible used to say Moses couldn't have written anything that long ago, because written language wasn't developed at that time.

But the library at Ebla dates about one thousand years *prior* to Moses. And although Ebla was a mostly pagan society, some of these Semitic tablets revealed all kinds of Hebrew tradition, including priestly codes, laws, ethics, sacrifices, and methods of worship (many of which, before this discovery, hadn't been believed to be in practice so long ago). The tablets also mention places like Sodom and Gomorrah and Jerusalem.

The library texts were written in two languages, Sumerian, and the majority being Semitic (later called Eblaite after this tablet, but it's similar to Hebrew). They even include multiple names for the one true God, plus common Hebrew names and a vocabulary that Moses still used a thousand years later. The creation account written in this text closely matches what Moses recorded.

So, it's reasonable to believe that Moses wrote the first five books of the Old Testament, each word inspired by God, confirming a long-established history of Hebrew tradition.

Critics also used to say it was "common knowledge" that monotheism (belief in one God) evolved out of supposed earlier beliefs of polytheism (belief in many gods) and henotheism (worshipping one god, but not denying there are many). The Ebla tablets proved, as far back as a thousand years before Moses, Jews believed One Being created everything out of nothing, contrary to all other mythical accounts of multiple gods and legendary, fantastic stories told in such ancient times. The Judeo-Christian God did not "evolve" from myths.

More recently, as reported by *Patterns of Evidence* and *The Times of Israel*, a city gate was discovered at Tel Erani in southern Israel that dates back 5,500 years—a huge gate serving as a fortified city entrance. This confirms urbanization was certainly going on long before Moses.

There have also been doubts about the Exodus of Jews out of Egypt (or Jews ever having been there). Archeology has once again substantiated the Bible. I found compelling evidence on the ABR site (Associates for Biblical Research) offering the top ten archeological finds supporting this major Biblical event (Brian Windle, Canadian pastor, article dated July 29, 2022). The list includes the following Egyptian evidence: Egyptian words in the original text that Moses wrote (a reminder of his Egyptian upbringing), early references to many Semitic/Hebrew names, images of brick-making in the manner the Hebrew slaves made them, the Egyptian Soleb inscription referring to the people of Yahweh, a pedestal with an Egyptian inscription now housed in Berlin which refers to the people of Canaan or "Ishrael," and finally the Merneptah Stele as a victory record for an Egyptian pharaoh winning a relatively minor attack against the people of "Israel" dated after the Hebrew's return from Egypt.

Skeptics even used to question whether Biblical figures like King David or Pontius Pilate actually lived, or if the Romans really did carry out such a horrible punishment as crucifixion. Not even the skeptics doubt these things any more, thanks to recent archeological finds.

- A dedication stone uncovered in 1961 dating from 26-36 AD named Pilate the prefect of Judea during this time. Also, a stamping ring found in 1969 that wasn't clearly read until 2018 with more advanced technology was inscribed with the name "Pilate." This unique item was found in the correct location and dates to the correct era. Other ancient historians such as Josephus (37 to 100 AD/CE) and Philo of Alexandria (25 BCE to 50 CE) also mention Pilate, so there's little doubt the Bible represented him correctly. Pilate is just one of the many correct proper names used in the Bible, from the people in power to the commonness of first names used during different eras and regions.

- King David goes back a long way (approximately 1000 BC), but in 1993 archeology uncovered the Tel Dan Inscription, a Canaanite stone that commemorates an Aramean king's victory over the "king of the House of David." Most scholars think the Aramean king refers to Hazael of Damascus when he defeated both Israel and the southern kingdom of Judah (remember, Israel split into two kingdoms after Solomon's reign, Israel to the north and Judah to the south).
- In 2021, archeologists uncovered a tassel and cloth fragments of "royal purple" dating back to 1000 BC, the time of David and Solomon's reign. This purple was drawn from snails and doesn't fade. Purple is described in Song of Songs 3:9-10, Ezekiel 27, Exodus 39, among others.
- Some skeptics doubted crucifixion was practiced, saying criminals were tied to trees with rope. However, heel bones of crucified victims (nail through the heel bone) were found in both the Middle East (1968) and Britain (2021) from when it was under Roman rule. This proves: one, that crucifixion in the way Christ was nailed to the cross was practiced, and two, criminals who suffered this practice were properly buried, contradicting claims Christ wouldn't have been allowed a proper burial because he was put to death as a "criminal."
- The Bible describes Jesus and later, the apostles, as going from town to town and teaching in synagogues,

inferring there were *many* synagogues so long ago in history. This was doubted until they kept finding more synagogues—two uncovered within 700ft. from one another in the ancient city of Magdala. (2009 and 2021)
- Erastus, referred by Paul in his letter to the Romans as a treasurer, has been proven an authentic historical figure. Archeologists uncovered a section of pavement crediting Erastus with having paid for this pavement at his own expense, indicating at the very least his personal wealth was separate from his civil service.

One source I read from the post *Atheist Reveals The Scientific & Historical Evidence That Converted Him To Christianity*, Justin Brooke, has a great presentation as to why copies of the Old Testament are so miraculously accurate. In antiquity, no less than the Library of Alexandria itself funded a high priest to oversee the translation of the Old Testament from original Hebrew to Greek two-hundred and fifty years before Christ was born. This version is called the Septuagint. The priest's name was Eleazor, and he commissioned seventy-two Hebrew scholars to do the job. This team worked under meticulous demands, even ordered to re-copy full pages if only the *spacing* between letters was off. After they finished their transcriptions, they were taken to separate rooms and made to precisely recite everything they'd transcribed. Only when all of them accurately recited the same words was their work confirmed as inspired by God.

There are many resources online detailing archeological finds that support the Bible's accuracy. From yearly "Top Ten" lists to more general "Biblical Archeology" you'll find a treasure trove of evidence. I highly recommend J. Warner Wallace videos, available on both YouTube and on his website, coldcasechristianity.com. He's a retired Forensics Detective (atheist turned Believer) and his general style of investigation appeals to Neil and me because it relies on evidence no matter the subject.

J. Warner used his cold case investigative skills to explore Christianity and the New Testament, looking for evidence to either reject or support the Bible. The following facts and questions define a cold case:

- The event is in the distant past.
- There are no living witnesses.
- Little or no forensic evidence remain.
- Is there convincing circumstantial evidence?

He made the point that in movies and on television, circumstantial evidence is often viewed dismissively. Actually, most convictions are gained using indirect, circumstantial evidence. If the cumulative circumstantial evidence all points in the same direction, a conviction usually follows. J. Warner allows the idea that while *anything is possible* (even hard to believe scenarios) *not everything is reasonable.*

Looking at the sources of Scripture much as he would have for any cold case file, J. Warner asked four questions:

- Are there any first hand witnesses?
- Are the witnesses reliable?
- Can witness accounts be corroborated?
- Do the witnesses have a bias?

At a crime scene, detectives ask these questions more specifically and personally to test potential witnesses:

- Can you verify they were actually **there**, at the scene?
- Are they **reliable**, or are they known by others to be untrustworthy?
- Are their accounts of what happened **accurate**? Do other accounts conflict or corroborate what they describe?
- Do they have a **bias** for or against what they're testifying?

Tracing the chain of custody with available ancient/Biblical text sources, we can verify whether or not a witness was present during or after Christ's life. The apostles, for example, are named as immediate sources in corroborating documents.

Were their accounts accurate, as compared with other contemporaneous or reliable accounts of the same events?

Is there other documentation putting their testimonies in doubt? Were they liars?

Were they biased?

About bias, J. Warner and Irish apologist Dr. John Carson Lennox say there are really only three motives for bias:

- Financial greed. Is there anything to gain?
- Sexual lust, crime of passion/gain sexual favor.
- Pursuit of power, or to gain respect or stature.

For the disciples, none of these motives can be suspected. They gained no wealth, in fact became itinerant preachers. There are no records of sexual promiscuity; they taught sexual purity to the new church. And they didn't gain power because it's well documented that early Christians were hunted and persecuted. Paul even lost power, since before following Christ he was an influential, honored and respected citizen of Rome. He ended up being hunted, much the same way he himself hunted Christians prior to his Damascus experience.

Is it possible there was some unknown motive for the disciples to spread the gospel, knowing it wasn't true, something we don't know about? Would the disciples and their followers have lied about Jesus' resurrection to protect Him and His ministry, to keep a greater good going? It's possible, but just not reasonable considering such a motive would have been based on a lie, contrary to what Jesus preached. Historical evidence from this era doesn't support a conspiracy theory. It's also likely at least one of the disciples/eyewitnesses involved in such a lie would have eventually revealed the truth, if only to save their own skin under rampant persecution against the new Christian movement.

———

As for the gospel writings themselves: how accurate are they? The disciples likely believed Jesus would come back in their lifetime, so perhaps they didn't see the urgency in producing duplicate documents in a time when oral traditions were more prevalent (most people couldn't read, and papyrus stores just weren't a thing back then!).

So besides having written his gospel, John went around preaching. He had many followers, or students, who learned this gospel through him. They, too, would have read and heard John's inspired message multiple times, and eventually shared it with students of their own. History can trace three of John's students, and at least two had students of their own (the third was imprisoned for his faith and history lost track of him). Ignatius is one of John's students, but the most familiar is Polycarp, John's student; Irenaeus and Tertullian were both students of Polycarp. Irenaeus then taught Hippolytus, which establishes an early "chain of custody," directly linking John's gospel to him as an original witness and writer. (Just Google "early church" to learn more about these old fellows.)

Through the lives of these "inheritors" of John's gospel as they copied and repeated, combining with the many, many copies of other original New Testament manuscripts (literally thousands), those who put our Bible together were able to compare the copies for a consistent message. The New Testament as known and accepted today derived from first century sources. The Council of Nicaea (AD 325) gathered most of the church's world leaders for the first time to settle on uniform doctrine, but our Bible wasn't officially listed as complete until 367 AD.

———

Timelines are important in investigations. J. Warner Wallace compared New Testament references within the Scriptures being used from the earliest times, verifying whether the timelines made sense. For example, the gospel of Luke refers to the gospel of Mark, so Mark must have been considered Scripture before Luke's. The Book of Acts, also written by Luke, refers to his gospel, so he wrote Acts after his Gospel of Luke.

J. Warner also looked for what *wasn't* mentioned in the prolific manuscripts used to write the final, accepted version. For example: the destruction of the temple in Jerusalem, which Jesus prophesied would fall, wasn't mentioned in the earliest retellings later considered Scripture. The first temple was erected under Solomon and destroyed when the Babylonians conquered Judah (Daniel was taken into exile in 605 BC by the Babylonians who destroyed the temple prior to that). The second temple was built under the reign of Cyrus (he's mentioned in the Prophecy segment of this book) around 538 BC. This second temple was expanded under Herod the Great, but came down during the Roman siege of Jerusalem in 69/70 AD. The siege and destruction of the temple were such major events that surely would have been included had the time of this telling and retelling been after these things happened. But it's not included, indicating the first accounts of these gospels and letters were written *before* this happened.

Also, James the son of Zebedee was put to death by Herod Agrippa only about 11 years after the death of Christ. This is recorded in Acts 12:1-2. Why wouldn't the deaths of *other* apostles be included if they were written after their deaths had occurred? Neither Paul's nor Peter's deaths are recorded, and both were martyred around 67 or 68 AD, just 30 or so years after Christ. Peter is said to have been crucified, and Paul was beheaded. Paul was a Roman citizen, therefore not eligible to suffer the horror of crucifixion. This would date many *original* gospel writings *before* 68 AD.

On the Gnostics

Although they are relatively ancient, Gnostic gospels weren't included in our Bible as Scripture because they weren't accepted by the earliest Christian traditions. The 39 books of the Old Testament were traditionally accepted more than 100 years before Christ was born. The New Testament books recognized each other's letters as Scripture during the lifetimes of the authors, as they are often referenced between them. They were recognized as authoritative by early churches relatively quickly.

As heretical texts came along, the church set out to preserve and protect what was already accepted as Scripture. Although the actual first letters written by the apostles were lost to decay, there were many, many copies made and circulated throughout the churches. Those copies were copied and copied and copied, then eventually compared and compared and compared to weed out as many discrepancies as possible. By the time the first official list of books for the New Testament was compiled in 367 AD it confirmed what was already in use.

But were the Gnostic gospels just overlooked?

No. They were rejected outright, because their theology didn't mesh with established doctrine from first generation Christians.

If someone wanted to embellish the truth, they would likely wait until most actual witnesses had died so none could dispute what they were spreading. This isn't the case for our New Testament. The letters to the Corinthians date as early as 53 AD, based on historical references and support from other Biblical texts. Some sources date Thessalonians even earlier than that. Either way, the first of Paul's letters to various new churches was written not long after he started preaching, and before some of the apostles were martyred.

If Jesus was crucified in approximately 33 AD, many Bible text authors were actual witnesses preaching to people who would also be witnesses to what had been going on at the time.

The Gnostic manuscripts were circulated hundreds of years

after eyewitnesses lived. The Gospel of Mary Magdalene, for example, was written hundreds of years after Mary's death.

The Gnostic books include so many quotes from established Scripture that most must have been written after New Testament teachings were already being circulated. Although some Gnostic books may have been written as early as 150 years after Christ, and the gospel of Thomas likely the earliest, none were written by contemporaries of Jesus or have anywhere near the amount of supporting evidence that New Testament Scripture offers.

Finally, the Gnostic manuscripts originate from the region of Egypt—far away from the witnesses and their offspring who would know the truth and refute any mythical embellishment. The only known town mentioned in Gnostic manuscripts from where Jesus and the apostles ministered is Jerusalem, unlike New Testament Scripture which names many towns from the region—too many to list, but you'd know them by the letters to authentic places like Corinth, Ephesus, Philippi, Colossae, etc..

The Gnostics also have few references to actual historical people, leaving out names like Caiaphas as High Priest, Herod as King and Pilate being Prefect, for example.

Plus, other proper names of those mentioned in these manuscripts include more Egyptian names, rather than those used exclusively from the Jewish region surrounding Jerusalem.

These are just a few of the basic reasons J. Warner gave for the Gnostic documents not being, and should not have been, included in our Bible.

Matthew, Mark, Luke and John are attributed to the content of each gospel because their books are the undisputed tradition and message each one of them originally wrote and preached. (Matthew, the tax collector from Jesus' day, Mark, or John Mark, who worked with Peter and Barnabas, Luke, probably a Gentile, a doctor and traveling companion to Paul, and John, the "Beloved Disciple" of Jesus.)

Here's a statement on Biblical authority from the Assemblies of God church: "The Scriptures, both Old and New Testaments, are verbally inspired of God and are the revelation of God to man, the infallible, authoritative rule of faith and conduct." Many churches have similar statements as a proclamation of faith that all authors of various books or letters in the Bible were inspired by God, not man.

Despite having lost the original documents to time, we trust God to have preserved the original inspiration He entrusted to each author. In support of that, we have more copies of the New Testament writings than any other ancient manuscript—thousands of copies, either complete or fragmented, in various languages. In Greek, there are 5,800. In Latin, 10,000. Various other languages (Syriac, Slavic, Gothic...) there are 9,300.

On variations between copies, or "Variants"

With so many copies available, scholars were able to do some of that "chain of custody" work to determine not only how early these copies date, but through comparison weed out variants. Almost all variants are so minor few people count them as concerning (i.e. using "He" rather than "Jesus" when it's obvious who the "He" is). These variants are usually noted in the footnotes in various versions of the Bible.

Some variants include the omission of certain words, or the order of words might vary within a sentence. Seventy percent of variants are simply differences in spelling.

Some variants are found only in a single copy, so those aren't considered important (or viable).

Less than 1% of variants are considered both meaningful and viable. However, even here, the variants don't change the message of Christ's ministry. For example, 1 John 1:4 refers to whose joy is complete in having written this letter. In some manuscripts it says "our joy" and others say "your joy" may be complete. The meaning is clearly different, since it talks about two different groups of people, but it doesn't change theology or put in question anything important other than the nice thought that somebody is going to receive joy for the creation and exchange of this letter.

Here's a note on variants as it pertains to witnesses: The Gospel of Matthew records Jesus, after His arrest and before his crucifixion, as being hit by the temple guards then challenged to prophesy as to who hit him (Matthew 26:67-68). Huh? Why would they taunt him to prophesy if one of the guards had just slugged him in front of everybody? It isn't until reading Mark 14:65 that we read Jesus had been blindfolded. Now it makes perfect sense. It's a variant, even an important detail, but doesn't change the gospel message or the nature of Jesus in any way.

Another reason to accept the accuracy of the New Testament is that the copies prove the gospel message didn't change over time. As J. Warner Wallace says at any crime scene: separate the witnesses so they can't collude on their story. There are always variants among eyewitnesses, but the truth is in what meshes. Lies, if there is a motive to tell any, usually change over time.

Even critics of the Bible who use variants as a reason to reject the Bible agree the variants don't change the message or meaning of the gospel. They may say there are simply too many variants to accept this Book as the "inerrant" Word of God, but for me, the miracle of so many copies working together to complete a single, consistent message about Christ's life, death and ministry, and the ministries He directly inspired, are just too close to perfect to worry about such minor details. Including the Old Testament, so many authors, so many eras, so many regions, all come together with one coherent message: of Jesus coming to save the world.

Conclusion: The gospels are largely testimonies of eye witnesses, the books of the New Testament have early dates, were originally inspired by God and written by the original authors, then copied thousands of times.

. . .

Outside historical and archeological support for the Bible

Other sources from antiquity mention Jesus and His ministry, apart from those who accepted Him as Deity. Thallus, in 52 AD, reported the earthquake and darkness that accompanied Christ's death on the cross.

Roman historian and scholar Cornelius Tacitus (56 AD-120 AD) referred to Pontius Pilate and the "mischievous superstition" surrounding Jesus called Christ, that He was crucified and his followers persecuted.

Phlegon (80-140 AD) stated Jesus had known the future, was no help to himself, and rose after death and showed his wounds.

Obviously, these weren't eyewitnesses and they weren't even Christians, however they reflect what was being talked about and generally believed at the time.

There are so many more, but in the interest of keeping this book short I won't go on too much longer. The book *Evidence That Demands a Verdict* has a far more extensive list of archeological discoveries that confirm the Bible, from Old Testament to New.

Speaking of McDowell's book...

Josh McDowell quotes C.S. Lewis from *Mere Christianity*. Lewis said you cannot call Jesus a great teacher and not accept His claim to be God. If He wasn't Who He *said* He was, then he couldn't have been a great teacher. He was either a lunatic or the devil or a fool. Only a fool would've surrendered His life for a lie or a delusion. Yet He was far too powerful a figure to have been a fool.

As McDowell famously expounds, Jesus was either a Lunatic, Liar or Lord. Either Jesus knew His claims to be God were false and lied or He believed them to be true and was delusional. If He was delusional, how could His ministry have been so effective? His teaching represented a deep understanding of Scripture, human nature and history. He was not only wise but savvy, shrewdly answering when others tried to trap Him with religious arguments. He attracted so many followers because of His love for all. (Just read the Sermon on the Mount!) He lived with calm assurance, with a profoundly simple message that pointed attention to heaven.

Jesus would have been a hypocrite if He was lying, because He admonished others to be honest. On top of that, if He assured His followers of a secure eternal life, but if He was actually lying, then He was like a demon for deceiving people about their eternity.

Jesus' disciples, actual witnesses, went into immediate hiding after the crucifixion. They feared the same fate. Yet upon Christ's resurrection they began to boldly preach the gospel. They also gave up sacred beliefs from their Jewish faith to adopt new ones as Christians, and not a single one abandoned these new beliefs even when persecuted or threatened with death.

Because the disciples followed Jesus, they gave up the following sacred Jewish traditions that had been in practice for 1500+ years (this paraphrased list came from *I Don't Have Enough Faith To Be An Atheist* by Geisler and Turek):

- Animal sacrifice, replaced by the belief that Jesus was the ultimate sacrifice.
- The supremacy of the Law of Moses; Jesus said He fulfilled the law, and He alone never broke any Law. Christians were set free of these laws.
- Absolute monotheism was replaced by worshipping Jesus, the God-man. Worshipping man was punishable by death under the Jewish faith.
- The Sabbath: to break it was also punishable by death. Most Believers no longer stuck to all the Sabbath rules.
- Prior to Jesus, faithful Jews believed in a Messiah who would conquer their oppressors (at the time, that would have been the Romans). But Jesus came meek and mild, a willing sacrifice. However, if you want to see a conquering Messiah, stick around for His second coming!

The disciples' lives and ministries—and their deaths—prove

they believed Him to be Lord. Why else would nearly all of them surrender their long-held traditions, even their life? For a Lunatic? A Liar? Or their Lord?

So, did Jesus actually say He was God?

In the Gospel according to Mark, the high priest Caiaphas bluntly asks Jesus if He's the Christ. Jesus says "I am," going further to say we'd see Him sitting on the right hand of power and coming in the clouds of heaven (second coming). Caiaphas, who knew his Old Testament Scripture, would have recognized this as a reference to Daniel's prophecy about the Son of Man coming to judge the world—an authority held only by God. For this, Jesus is called a blasphemer because everyone knew what He was saying: He's God.

In the Gospel according to John, Jesus says "before Abraham was born, I am!" Was this just bad grammar? No, Jesus was calling Himself one of the names God called Himself, the name that caught my husband's attention because of its timelessness. He was, is, and is to be. He's the Great I Am.

That's why the Jews of Jesus' day crucified Him, because they knew He claimed to be God.

The Bible also holds a number of indirect claims that Jesus is God. These are a few instances, paraphrased from Geisler's and Turek's book:

- In Revelation Jesus says He is the first and the last, the Alpha and the Omega. (Revelation 1:8 and 1:17) This is what God called Himself in Isaiah 44:6.
- John 10:11 Jesus calls Himself the Good Shepherd. God is the Shepherd in the famous 23rd Psalm.
- In Matthew, Jesus claimed to be the judge of all people. (Matthew 25:31-46) Only God is the judge.
- Jesus said He is the Light of the world (John 8:12) but the Psalms say The Lord (meaning God) is my light (Psalm 27:1)

- When Jesus healed the paralytic in Mark 2:5-11, He said "Son, your sins are forgiven." For that He was accused of claiming to be God, because only God can forgive sins. (Isaiah 43:25)
- Jesus asked us to pray in His name. (John 14:13)
- Jewish tradition strictly forbids any worship of man. Yet Jesus accepted worship from others, among them those whom He healed, and my favorite, Thomas, who evidently wasn't around on resurrection day. Others told him about Jesus being raised, but Thomas said he wouldn't believe it until he touched Jesus' scars. Jesus obliged by showing up. Thomas fell to his knees and said "My Lord and My God." (John 20:28) If Jesus wasn't God, and if Jesus didn't want others to recognize Him as God, He could have done what angels did in other instances when they show up in front of mere mortals who often want to worship them. The Bible records the angel in Revelation saying to John, "Don't worship me! That's only for God!" (Revelation 22:9) Surely if Jesus didn't want Thomas breaking any Jewish laws about worshiping something other than God, He would have pulled Thomas to his feet and said, "Only worship God, Tom! Come to your senses and get to your feet!" But He didn't contradict Thomas at all, because He is, in fact, God.

Jesus' sinless life, the miracles He performed, and His resurrection all point to Him being God. Still, He could have just stood on the Mount of Olives and shouted "Hey! I'm God!" Would that be clear enough?

Only if you wanted to create new problems. Remember, this was Jesus' first coming. If He'd been that overt about His claims, people naturally would have tried at the very least to put a crown on His head. They also would have expected Him to get rid of the big bullies from Rome.

But He had a different purpose in His first coming. Was He supposed to remind them of his Deity every time He wanted to gather His flock? We saw in His forty days in the desert that He wasn't going to use His power in a way that would help Him or even save Him from pain. Then when the crucifixion happens . . . well, that was His whole purpose, wasn't it? He wanted to give evidence of who He was as Messiah and Savior, but not so overwhelmingly that it wouldn't still take faith to believe in Him.

As mentioned above, Jesus never broke any of the Laws that God set in place. Recently on the site *Patterns of Evidence*, I read about a challenge to the Mosaic Laws accusing Moses of copying the laws, or at least some of them, from an already existing Mesopotamian list uncovered in an archeological dig in the 1950s and '60s. The Mesopotamian and Babylonian relics are older than the date Moses was to have written God's laws.

The biggest crimes are similarly forbidden by all three cultures, like murder, stealing, adultery, rape. All three cultures also have a "measure for measure" retribution system, i.e. "an eye for an eye" type of thing. If a man murders, he shall be put to death.

Here's why those similarities shouldn't come as a surprise: God didn't just give Moses and His people a conscience. It's written on *all* our hearts because we're made in God's image. (Romans 2:14-16) The Mesopotamians and Babylonians would have known this instinctively. Many of the laws Moses recorded had existed since the beginning, as recorded in his historical book of Genesis.

Every culture establishes rules to thrive, including isolated tribes today around the world which have similar rules. It doesn't mean their culture copied from older ones. It's evidence of our universal conscience.

The fact that these artifacts date older than Moses' lifetime doesn't predate existing traditions upon which these laws were given.

Secondly, the differences are also important. I won't take the time to present and defend the many Mosaic laws since Jesus set us free from such things, but historically speaking, as antiquated as many of the Mosaic laws are, especially filtered through a modern lens, Mosaic law showed God's love for all mankind. But in these other ancient laws, a person could receive the death penalty even for property crimes. Or, if the victim was from the higher class, the punishment would be greater than if the victim was poor or a culturally insignificant commoner. Overall, rich men were treated better than women, poor men, children or slaves while Mosaic law didn't generally consider class.

Thirdly, the authority behind the sets of laws also makes a difference. Moses wrote those laws with the authority of God. The other two mentioned were written with the authority of their kings, in one case Hammurabi and in the Mesopotamian case Ur-Nammu. It could reasonably be argued that these kings not only wanted to establish order, but they also wanted to exercise their own authority and hang on to power. Moses' law, on the other hand, gave the authority to God with a set of rules meant to protect all mankind for a safe and fruitful future.

As you can see from this limited selection, there are many archeological discoveries that confirm the historical accuracy of the Bible. Let this be a start if you'd like to do more "digging" on your own. I look forward to learning more historical evidence in the future!

SCIENCE

In this chapter, my husband Neil and I will present our beliefs about how the Bible is a partner, not an opponent, of science. While we admit other sections may lift a brow or two, even from Christians, we anticipate this chapter may be the most controversial among our fellow Christ-followers and secular friends alike.

Many of our secular friends will agree to disagree about various points in this chapter, but let's start with what Christians largely agree about:

- The Bible's Creation account stands alone as incredibly accurate in its chronology, specifically, the order of what happened in the Earth's and Universe's history.
- While some of the first chapter in Genesis may sound poetic in its language and rhythm, the Creation account is not a poem, myth, or allegory.
- The Bible's Creation account places the Creator outside of energy, space, matter and time. In other words, God created everything out of nothing, including the laws of physics. He wasn't subject to such things. This is unique to Christianity.

- God created Adam and Eve as fully human, and every human alive today is a descendant of them.
- The exquisite fine-tuning of the Universe demands an investigation as to whether it could be a random event via physical means only.

Where we differ:

- Either the original seven days of creation represent seven, twenty-four-hour days, or are seven consecutive eras of time. Both sides believe in a literal reading of Scripture.
- Death and suffering (of plants and animals) occurred before Adam and Eve disobeyed God.

Although there are twice as many points of agreement, the two differences may seem insurmountable. It's probably a good moment for us to remember that even the deepest held differences on this subject aren't the "eternity" kind of difference. In other words, we all agree on those core basics I mentioned in the Preface about our Savior, Jesus Christ, being the only way to heaven (John 14:6) through His redemptive sacrifice on the cross (1 Peter 2:24), and the Bible is the Truth with a capital T (2 Timothy 3:16).

As part of the Church, we'd do well to remember John Carson Lennox's view on this topic when debates rise among Believers. How do we, as the united Body of Christ, handle our differences? Our job is to represent our loving Creator, and we can't do that well without grace.

Dr. Lennox reminds us the church once believed the earth was immovable (1 Chronicles 16:30 and Psalm 93:1, to name a couple). Then Copernicus and Galileo came along, and over time it became indisputable that the earth is moving through space. Is Scripture wrong?

As you'll see in this chapter, the answer is in perspective. If you're standing on the face of the earth, as all of us are, Earth does indeed feel "immovable" just as Scripture describes it to be. Earth is also "fixed" in its place within our solar system, though Earth is moving at 67,000 mph around the sun, and our solar system is moving around the center of the Milky Way Galaxy and our galaxy is moving away from other galaxies as the Universe expands. You can only say an object is not moving if you share the same motion, such as standing still on the earth.

Dr. Lennox believes, as do all Christians, in the authority of Scripture, and understanding these verses from this perspective makes sense. These verses could also be read as figure of speech, affirming the permanence of God's will on creation.

The point is, the Bible's account of creation can be earnestly interpreted either as seven long eras *or* as 24-hour creation days. We needn't be dogmatic in one view or the other. In other words, give some grace to our brothers and sisters in Christ who differ on this interpretation. We all love and serve the same God, Jesus.

A different-than-twenty-four-hour day isn't a new idea created to accommodate modern science. It's been the subject of pondering since the first century by Christians and Jews alike. In his book *A Matter of Days*, Hugh Ross lists scholars from the first through fourth centuries, starting with Jewish scholar Philo and ending with Augustine, who proposed different periods of time for the days listed in Genesis. For example, Philo thought God created everything instantaneously, that each day was meant to explain the *order* of things as God created them. Whether or not Philo was right about an instantaneous creation for everything, the Bible is miraculous in exactly this way, that it does perfectly explain the chronology for God's creation event.

Second century scholars Justin Martyr and Irenaeus (we met the latter in the last chapter as a student of Polycarp who learned from the Apostle John) drew from Scripture that a "day" could be epochs. (Psalm 90:4 and 2 Peter 3:8 say a thousand years is like a day to the Lord.) Clement of Alexandra was in Philo's camp, though he lived a hundred years later. Clement agreed the days represented the order and priority but not the time for each creation step.

A fellow named Origen (185-254 AD) thought the *spiritual meaning* of the creation account, actually of all Scripture, is the proper interpretation. He claimed time as we know it didn't exist until the fourth day. He finishes by saying the last day, the one where God rested after creation ended with the pinnacle of Adam and Eve, won't end until God brings His current creation to an end. He'll then create again to make a new heaven and new Earth.

And finally Augustine, who said the creation days were not like our days, that the mornings and evenings were figurative. He reminded us that the seventh day had no evening or morning so he, like Mr. Origen, believed that day extended far longer than twenty-four hours; Augustine believed this last day extends into eternity.

Speaking of old-timers and their opinions on the age of the Universe, none of the early Christian creeds (a consensus of core doctrine to weed out heretical teaching) include how long each creation day lasted. We might assume that's because they all thought they were seven, twenty-four-hour periods. However, consider the following information I read in Ross's book (*A Matter of Days*) referring to the time shortly after the King James Bible translation was first printed:

In the year 1642, Cambridge University Vice-Chancellor John Lightfoot studied genealogies in Genesis, Exodus, both books of Kings, and both books of Chronicles. He concluded the initial Creation day was September 17, 3928 BC. He ignored Hebrew scholars whose work claimed there were missing generations in these various genealogies.

Eight years later, an Irish Anglican archbishop corrected Lightfoot's date to October 4, 4004 BC. A year, by the way, far easier to read, say and remember!

Lightfoot ultimately went along with the 4004 BC year, but said the actual day was October 23rd at 9:00 a.m..

I've written a historical romance or two with characters from England and Ireland, and these two notable men came from countries which have provided many authors the potential for conflict through lineage. Maybe Lightfoot and Ussher were trying to outdo one another in their precision simply because one was Irish and the other English. But I digress.

We can giggle at these meticulous dates, particularly the 9:00 a.m. part, but unfortunately the fact that future editions of the King James Version included the 4004 BC date as fact in margin notes or subject headings was the beginning of not only common doctrinal beliefs but some serious contention about the length of creation days. Ussher, because he was the first of the two to claim 4004 BC as the year, is credited with this as the creation date discovery.

Before and after Ussher, few churches considered this question as important to the basic Gospel message. In fact, even among those who believe the Universe is young, today concede there were likely some missing generations in the Biblical accounts. They have adjusted their creation date as anywhere from 6,000 to 10,000 years ago.

By 1857 when geological evidence pointed more and more toward a much older Earth, Christians in scientific fields needed to come to terms with these facts based on what they believed from the authority of the King James Bible. The 4004 BC Creation date was clearly noted in the versions they read, and was hard to separate from actual Scripture. (My KJV edition dates to 1962 and no such headings or notes existed by that point.) Anyway, a British biologist and preacher named Philip Gosse published his idea that God created the Earth with the appearance of age. Sure, it *looks* really, really, really old, but God actually created it a few thousand years ago. After all, He created Adam as a fully grown man, didn't He? On Adam's first day of life, he appeared much older than he was. Gosse's book generated some early interest but the idea faded—maybe because people came away with the same feeling I had when I heard it. Why would God try fooling us into seeing it as old, but it's really young? Creating Adam as fully grown was necessary for his survival, whereas creating stars billions of light years away is another matter altogether.

What's so puzzling to me is that many of those insisting the

Universe is young do so for the same reason I hold an old Earth belief: because what the Bible says is the final, ultimate authority. We may call Nature another way God has revealed Himself to us as a loving, personal and generous God, but that in no way usurps what it reveals about God through Scripture. One enhances the other. I hold to *sola Scriptura*, meaning the Bible stands alone as having been written with the full authority of God. If nature contradicts the Word of God, there's a misinterpretation somewhere and demands investigation.

Dr. Ross compares our present contention about long or short creation days to the vehemence early Jewish Believers in Christ held about circumcision. The early church responded by reminding everyone of the salvation issue—core beliefs they all shared. Why make it more difficult for Gentiles to be saved, since Jesus didn't command circumcision from the broader range of His followers? The early church handled that issue with grace.

Officially, the first council to discuss these differences was the International Council on Biblical Inerrancy (ICBI) in 1982. They listened to representatives from both sides as well as a scholar to analyze Genesis's original language. The panel ultimately decided that a belief in seven consecutive twenty-four-hour days was not an essential perspective for belief in the inerrancy of the Bible. They put together a formal conclusion stating as much, and everyone except the young Earth representative was willing to sign it. He insisted they rephrase the document so generically that it wouldn't offend those who strictly believe the Earth to be young. I suppose because the document ended up so generic, it was largely ignored and has been out of print for about thirty years.

Since then, the Presbyterian Church in America (PCA) and the Westminster Theological Seminary have presented both young and old Earth perspectives as valid and shouldn't divide any of their congregations. Ross's book was originally published almost twenty years ago, but even today this sort of openness isn't seen very widely, if the subject is brought up at all.

There are a number of prominent Christians who believe in an old Earth, and that number is growing, but to many Christians this isn't an area to either lose friends or sleep over. It's my prayer that those who hold one side or the other won't label the other side as satanically deceived. I'm firmly convinced once we're in heaven these kinds of differences will disappear along with myriad other conflicts that are far too common in our fallen world.

Definition of "Day"

As Dr. Ross reminds us, the word "yom" or "yowm" in the Bible can be interpreted a few different ways: for part of the daylight hours, for all of the daylight hours, for a full twenty-four hour period, or for long but finite periods of time. It's important to realize the Hebrew language has far fewer words than English or Greek, so many Hebrew words have to do at least double-duty.

In Genesis 2:4, "in the day that the Lord God made the earth and the heavens" (KJV) clearly refers to "day" as more than one twenty-four-hour-day even if you hold each of the creation days were twenty-four-hours.

In the Book of Hebrews, (4:1-11) we're invited to rest with God *today*, reminding us of His rest continuing after creation. This suggests the seventh day of rest is lasting until "today." The brackets defining the beginning and end of that seventh day are missing, implying the day didn't end.

The important thing is that this word isn't bound to one definition.

More on the length of days

As Dr. Frank Turek notes, the Genesis account of creation could also represent, as other portions of Scripture do, a poetic reflection of what was going on with God's chosen people at the time, even though it's far more than poetry. The important thing, he says, is to note the amazing chronological order of creation. The Genesis account simply doesn't give details as to how long each creation event took, because the "evening and morning" references are poetic repetitions marking the beginning and end of each period of time, no matter how long that period of time might be. (Ancient custom was to count the beginning of one day in the evening and go twenty-four hours from there.)

In addition, Turek reminds us that Moses wrote the first five books of the Bible (the Pentateuch) after leading the Jews out of Egypt. This creation account not only reveals what God did and the order in which He did it, but refutes what the Egyptian accounts said of creation at the time: that gods who do not predate everything around us (as the Hebrew God does) brought order to chaos. By contrast, God told Moses to let everyone know He was *outside* of creation because He created everything out of nothing. (Genesis 1:1, Psalm 33:9, Isaiah 44:24 & 45:12, Romans 4:17, Colossians 1:16, Hebrews 11:3)

Also from *A Matter of Days*, Hugh Ross presents a compelling argument against one objection to longer days I've heard first hand: any little old grandma who picks up the Bible for the first time should be able to understand it simply. Therefore, a simple understanding of the Genesis creation event says everything was created in "7 days" so "7 days" it is, as any little old granny would understand a twenty-four-hour day to mean.

However, there are countless passages that need not only pondering but deep theological study. Like: who were the Nephilim? And am I literally not supposed to wear gold jewelry as it says in 1 Peter 3:3? Don't even get me started on the impossibility of understanding Old Testament laws or the Book of Revelation. Anyway, Ross refers to "Alice" who picked up a Bible for the first time as a young woman. She observed that Adam and Eve were created on the same busy sixth day of creation, which is described in more detail in the second chapter of Genesis. Eve was created *after* both God and Adam completed several other tasks that day:

- God planted a garden and all kinds of trees, and introduced Adam to it after placing him in the garden.

- God instructed Adam to care for the Garden of Eden.
- God instructed Adam to name all the animals.
- Adam realized none of the animals were a good companion for him, indicating a sense of loneliness.
- God performed surgery on Adam, taking one of his ribs (or a portion of his side), and created Eve.

Alice's simple reading told her this was a lot to do in twenty-four-hours. Besides, she noticed with Augustine about the seventh day of creation not having the brackets of "evening and morning," suggesting the seventh day never ended. She thought perhaps each of the previous days weren't twenty-four-hour periods, either. Fast forward in Alice's life to when she became a grandma. She read about scientific discoveries and the age of the Universe, and none of it challenged her faith in the Bible's accuracy.

More specifically, Ross notes when Adam saw Eve for the first time in Genesis 2:23 he says "Happa'am." It's a Hebrew word also mentioned in Genesis 30:20 and Genesis 46:30 as "now," in KJV (with a sense of time passage), "at last" and "finally" in the NLT and CSB versions. It paints a picture of Adam going through many animals and growing lonely and eager for a companion, which is more appropriate for a longer sense of time than just a few hours.

Before we get into more technical "sciency" stuff, I thought it would be a good idea to explain how an old earth perspective aligns with the seven Creation Days in the Bible. It's one of the best examples of how extraordinary the Bible really is. I learned most of this material from Hugh Ross's work, either from his excellent and easy-to-read book, *A Matter of Days*, or from listening to his many YouTube videos. I'm going to keep to the first chapter of Genesis as the most familiar description, even though there are many other creation accounts in Scripture (in Job and Psalms, for example).

. . .

In the Beginning...

The very first verse in Genesis says God created the Heaven and the Earth. This is the Big Bang. Poof! There was nothing, and then there was something. A straightforward reading of the verse reveals the beginning of the Universe as created in an instant and eventually Earth, by God who is outside of this realm.

God is already at work establishing the constant laws that rule the Universe (like gravity, etc.). This starting point is extremely hot, but that heat was needed to create certain elements throughout the Universe that are necessary to sustain life, even today. God was planning for a time in cosmic future when Earth would become a friendly, stable environment for us. If an old age for Earth demonstrates anything, it's how patient God is!

The second verse in Genesis states the Earth was without form and empty (or void, if you're a KJV enthusiast). Darkness was upon the face of the deep. And the Spirit of God moved upon the face of the waters. This is an accurate portrait of Earth in its earliest stage. It was empty. It was dark. It was covered with water. The perspective here is from God as He "moves" or "hovers" just above Earth's water. He's no longer outside looking down on what He'd summoned into existence by His Word, He's describing to Moses who wrote Genesis the vantage Moses would've had from Earth's surface.

The reason Earth is dark, even though God has already created the Universe (including the sun, moon, stars and the rest of the planets) is that the atmosphere around Earth is so thick none of the light can penetrate to reach the surface, where God is hovering. The light couldn't have been seen from Earth. As Dr. Ross explained in one of his frequent visits to universities and churches all over the world, our atmosphere at this time in history was a lot like that of Venus, too thick to let in any light.

Day One

Verse three in Genesis quotes God as saying: Let there be light.

Notice the words aren't "Then God created light." He said "*Let there be light, and there was light.*" This refers to the clearing away of some space debris that had yet to settle into place. This thinned our atmosphere enough so at least some light could reach the surface of the already-created Earth.

After this, in Genesis 1:4, God divides the light, and in the fifth verse calls light Day and darkness Night. The atmosphere is thin enough to let in some of the light during the day, and as the Earth rotates on its axis, it's darker at night. This era ends with the same language used after every creation event: And the evening and the morning were the first day. This is a clear bracket to define the beginning and ending of the first day, or era as I understand it. This bracket is repeated through the sixth day but left out from the seventh.

Day Two

In the sixth verse God again uses the phrase "Let there be" rather than "created." He says to "let there be a firmament" (sky, heavens or, specifically, the troposphere) in the midst of the waters, separating the "waters from waters" (separating out our various forms of water: rain, mist, dew, snow, frost and hail). God is establishing the just-right conditions Earth needs for an efficient, abundant and stable water cycle.

Day Three

Let the waters under the heaven be gathered together . . . and let dry land appear. After the waters receded, He "brought forth" (or created) all kinds of plants and trees and grass. The plants and trees and grass are new, but the land was already there. It had just been under the water but now the land is appearing because the waters are gathering into oceans and seas. This perfectly aligns with the history of Earth, that, over time, the plate tectonics moved and ocean basins formed so the seas became defined. It wasn't until roughly the year 2000 that science verified what the Bible already told us: Earth was once completely covered with water, before shifting plates pushed up land and lowered sea floors.

Day Four

Let there be lights in the heaven, meaning God thinned out the atmosphere even further so that it can be translucent and ultimately transparent (well, at least when it's not foggy or rainy or snowy or . . . you get the picture). From atop the newly emerged continents, you can finally see through our atmosphere to observe not just the light from the sun, but now even the stars and the light reflected off the moon to be seen through our atmosphere, too. The chronology here is important, because God knew the next phase of creation would need a more obvious sense of time as defined by our days and nights (which previously would have been nearly indistinguishable due to the lingering thickness of the atmosphere).

Day Five

The Avalon Explosion! Making way for the Cambrian Explosion! (More on these explosions later.) On Day Three God had already created plenty of vegetation, and on Day Four He let the clock by which animals need to set their routines, day and night, to be clearly experienced. So here they start coming, small sea animals, birds, and sea mammals, including whales. The text actually uses the same word as in verse one, "created." Many of the earliest life forms went extinct so we'd have fossil fuels today, but not to worry! Day Six is next.

Day Six

After having created birds and sea animals, God now "makes" land mammals that would later interact with humans (not just wild animals but also farm animals and pets). Sure, there were more rocky days ahead including more extinction events (good-bye Dino the Dinosaur) but throughout this phase of Earth's history, God created every species we know today. The fossil record showing this explosion of life over a relatively short period of time (short, by geological terms, but millions of years) is one of the biggest obstacles Darwinists face. We may agree on some small changes (microevolution) but there have been no new groups of unique species created (macroevolution) since the Cambrian Explosion.

God finishes this busy day by creating Adam and Eve, the pinnacle of His creation. I say pinnacle because He didn't send His son to die for animals or even angels, whose creation isn't mentioned in the creation day chronology. Jesus came to save just us.

Day Seven

God rests, and because there are no brackets clearly defining a beginning and end to this period of time, God is still resting from creating anything new. He will, however, create one more time when He replaces the present heaven and Earth with new ones after the Millennium Age (Revelation 21:1, Isaiah 65:17).

Here's a concise list of the ten creation events, some during the same day/era but happening over a gradual period of time:

1. God created the entire Universe and then Earth. (Genesis 1:1)
2. God cleared away the cosmic debris and partially thinned out the atmosphere so some of the sun's light could reach Earth.
3. God formed the troposphere, setting up our water cycle in the atmosphere closest to Earth.
4. He formed ocean basins and continents.
5. God created plants on the land masses.

6. He transformed our atmosphere to the translucent or sometimes transparent one we have today.
7. Created lots of small sea animals.
8. Created birds and sea mammals.
9. Created land mammals that would one day serve and enrich human life.
10. Created Adam and Eve.

This is from Hugh Ross's book *A Matter of Days*. The order of these ten creation events are chronologically listed in the Book of Genesis, each one miraculously reported in the correct order that we know today, 3,400 years later. The fact that this list is correct 10 for 10 and written by Moses so long ago is too incredible to ignore, setting the Bible apart from every other religious book.

About the rain

Certain sedimentary records show splash patterns of rain, so rain did fall on Earth long before God created Adam and Eve. But how can I justify Genesis 2:5-6 about God not having sent rain yet, and springs (or mists) watering the land?

These verses confirm the state of the Earth before God set the water cycle (troposphere) in place (Day 2, above). After the water cycle is established, God brings forth the land by settling the water into lakes and oceans, etc., then later creates Adam and Eve to tend the Garden. So there was no rain during Earth's earliest phase. In Job 38 when God reminds Job of creation, God mentions the water cycle He put into place, including rain. There is no gap between creation and the first rainfall in this retelling, even though a significant number of years would have passed between Adam and Noah. This and other references about creation in Psalms 104 and 108 talk about rain or snow and clouds, without separating such weather from the original act of supernatural creation.

I'm reminded that God used the rainbow as a covenant, promising He would never again destroy mankind by flood. That's why I love rainbows, because they remind me of God, just as His covenants are meant to do! But does this mean there were no rainbows, and thus no rain, before this? What about communion, when He used bread and wine to remind us of Jesus' sacrificed Body and Blood? God used something already in existence, and familiar, to remind us of His promise that through Jesus' death on the cross we can receive God's grace. There's really no need for the rainbow to have been brand new when He used it as a reminder of His promise.

There you have the framework for my perspective on how the Biblical account of creation matches to an amazing degree what science has since learned about the history of our Universe and Earth. Even though some friends and loved ones holding a young earth view might have been tolerant enough to read this information, I don't expect to change anyone's mind. And that's okay because, as I said at the outset, this is a presentation of why I believe what I believe. This is one of those perspectives that we can agree to disagree on. We'll forget all about these kinds of differences when we're feasting together in heaven.

Neil and I have more scientific details to come that support our beliefs (as you might guess from the length of this section) but first I'd like to address philosophical differences that separate the two camps, young or old Earth.

One of the common philosophical reasons to reject an old Earth

Death before the fall. When I listen to young earth enthusiasts talk about creation, they refer to God looking over His work and calling it "perfect." Only after man sinned did Earth become less than perfect. Laws of science, which the Bible calls the fixed laws (Jeremiah 33:25) must have been different before sin entered this perfect environment.

And if the Garden was perfect, there would have been no death at all. No pain for Eve in childbirth nor struggle for Adam as he farmed the perfect soil of Eden.

However, the text actually calls creation "good." It doesn't say perfect. Perfect, I'm convinced, is reserved for our eternal future.

Nonetheless, death before Adam and Eve's sin is a big hurdle for some, perhaps until realizing the concept of death before the fall would apply only to plants and animals. In other words, death certainly did come through one man, Adam, and was conquered through another man, Jesus. However, I believe death after the fall applies to those made in God's image: mankind's physical as well as the spiritual death sin brings.

From an excellent chapter in Hugh Ross's book *A Matter of Days*, "Good God, Cruel World," here are a couple questions Dr. Ross inspired about God's intention when He created Adam and Eve:

- If all death is strictly tied to evil, then is death evil?
- Why would Adam's sin result in punishment not only for himself and Eve and all their offspring right down to you and me, but also for all plants and animals even though they didn't do anything to deserve this new punishment?

Plant Death before Adam and Eve

Since the Bible states that even plants and animals (including non-soulish animals) experience life and death, it's reasonable to include this sort of death as pertinent to the topic of death before Adam and Eve. The Old Testament records the deaths of fishes, frogs, plants which died from locusts, even flies. So the definition of "death" does effect such lower life forms.

As Dr. Ross reminds us, any sort of work or movement God expected of Adam and Eve would have required energy from the beginning. All energy takes an energy source: food. Even before the fall, Adam and Eve ate. Even if they didn't eat meat, plants would have died in order to sustain the first human couple until the serpent approached Eve—we don't know how much time passed between the sixth day of creation and the fall, but it's fairly obvious Adam and Eve ate something natural (since there is no mention of something like manna, the supernatural food source God provided after Moses led the Jews out of Egypt and back to the Promised Land of Israel after years of slavery).

Animal Death before Adam and Eve
Even if creation days were only twenty-four-hours, according to Hugh Ross there are and have been in existence since the first creation day certain species that couldn't even live three hours without eating (additional example of the death of plants, at least).

Animals aren't very picky about the plants they eat, and it's likely there would have been insects on some of those ingested plants way back nearer the beginning. Have you ever had the disgusting experience of biting into a peach only to find a worm? Worse, half a worm? So certain small animals were likely eaten by other animals, if only by mistake. As Dr. Ross points out, huge elephants probably stepped on unsuspecting little bugs.

On the other hand, if you exclude these kinds of deaths and attributed the punishment of death because of Adam to only "soulish" animals like birds and mammals (possessing mind, will and emotions) then these are included in suffering death through sin. Yet Scripture says only humans deserve to be called sinners. Romans 5 describes death coming to "all men" through Adam, leaving out entirely any reference to plants or animals.

Jesus' sacrifice was for all mankind, not for animals, suggesting a stark difference between the death of animals and man. Only humans are referenced as being "made alive in Christ," for eternity, not animals. (One caveat here, since there will be animals in heaven, I'm open to the idea that God may bring our favorite pet back to life for eternity, but that's a whole 'nuther book.)

In various parts of the Bible, it says animals receive their prey from God (Job 38:39-41, Psalm 104:21, for example). How can this kind of animal death be an evil result of man's sin, since it appears God condones it?

Why blame Adam for all death and decay in the Universe when he wasn't even the first sinner? The serpent was the first culprit, so casting all the blame for plant, animal and mankind's death forgets the actual history of sin.

Some of my young earth friends will remind me of the verse, also in Romans (Chapter 8) that the whole earth "groans" in wait of the day it, too, will be free of death and decay, suffering since Adam's original sin. I believe when God assigned Adam to "tend" the garden, it still meant he'd need to work at it, even inside Eden. As Dr. Hugh Henry and Daniel J. Dyke point out in their excellent article "What Does A 'Very Good' World Look Like?" berries will still grow on vines whether tended or not, but they'll grow more abundantly when tended. And so, when God said Adam should "subdue" and "rule" over every living thing, he was meant to tame something that wasn't, from the beginning, supernaturally going to live up to its own potential, even inside Eden. Work wasn't part of the curse, even though the Garden of Eden might have had ideal growing conditions. Once Adam and Eve were thrown out, there would be *increased* struggle to tend subsequent gardens and animals. It's also possible Adam didn't quite enjoy the work as much as he did over a garden planned and planted by God Himself.

My point is that the conditions on Earth didn't change because of Adam's original sin. He worked before sin, and worked after, only the work became harder, perhaps at least in part because his broken relationship with God hovered over tasks Adam once more thoroughly enjoyed.

On suffering

It's a dramatic comparison to link sin with blood, but that seems to be what the Bible does. Undoing sin demands a heavy price because God isn't just good, He's perfect. But Hebrews 10:1-4 explain that the blood of animals from Old Testament sacrifices didn't take away sin; those sacrifices were a reminder of the seriousness of sin and as a forerunner to the ultimate sacrifice to be paid for all sin: Jesus' blood on the cross. Although sin brought physical death to mankind, Jesus saved us from an eternal spiritual death.

Pain must have existed before the fall, if only as part of our own physical protection. Surely Adam and Eve had a sense of touch, but that means being able to feel the burn if you get too close to fire.

And when God said to Eve that her pain would "multiply" in child birth, that must have meant she had at least some pain to begin with. Again, we don't know how much time passed between creation and the fall, so it's possible Eve had already experienced childbirth before eating the forbidden fruit. Whether that event was past or future, if the original plan was zero pain, multiplying zero by any number would still be zero.

To Adam He said his work would be *harder*, implying it was never without some challenge, as I talked about above. The laws of science didn't change when Adam and Eve sinned or the record of this planet would show a change since science can trace history long before God created man. What changed was that the more mankind sins, the more pain we face and the harder work becomes on a decaying planet.

Let's visit a brief history of science.

Here's a shout-out to early Muslims, who seemed eager to explore science (scientific method/mathematics/medicine, among other areas). But even while their conquests were on the rise, Muslims began pulling away from scientific exploration. Anti-philosophical sentiments spread among their largest sect (the Sunnis) and that was the end of scientific discovery. Ultimately, even science leads to philosophy.

Science as we know it today really took off during Europe's

"Enlightenment" phase of history, and has continued ever since. Most of the founders of modern science were Christians. If they weren't, their European setting was certainly dominated by Christianity. It would take an entirely different book to discuss how politics corrupted the church at various times, or how many atheists during the Enlightenment wanted to replace God with science. But many of the founding fathers of European scientific method wanted to investigate our world to know God's creation better. In some ways, their exploration of our natural world was an act of worship.

Let's just say this: if it weren't for Christian patrons during this era, either funding individuals or opening universities, few of the scientists we know today would have had the means to live their lives exploring the world around us. The Christians we know best are Galileo, Bacon, Kepler, Pascal and Newton, but there are many, many others!

Believe it or not, scientists once thought they "knew it all." Isaac Newton published his Principia in 1687 which contained his 3 laws of motion (ask Neil about those, and he'll not only give you definitions, he'll lead you through lab experiments). Newton also published the Universal Theory of Gravity that attempted to explain the motion of all visible bodies in the Universe. After these breakthroughs, physics seemed to be wrapping it up and running out of research direction. At the time, they believed we lived in an eternal, static (unchanging) Universe that was behaving nicely and providing an environment suitable for life on earth.

Skip forward to Lord Kelvin, who stated in 1900: "There is nothing new to be discovered in physics now. All that remains is more and more precise measurement."

Darwin had published his *On the Origin of Species* in 1859. In that, he laid out how mutations and natural selection were responsible for changes in all living beings—from protozoa to upright homosapiens to modern day man. He claimed branches from one common descent led to the diversity of life we've ended up with today.

Neil and I acknowledge evolution is a tough subject because for so long schools haven't allowed any alternatives to Darwin's theory. Culturally, both micro- and macroevolution are granted as facts, and many intelligent people are convinced the scientific community has settled or will settle this issue in favor of Darwin's theory. We acknowledge the lack of depth described here with regards to this (or other topics included), but our goal is to give a glimpse into the foundation of our beliefs. Keeping an open mind as science reveals more complexity about life and its origins demands further study from all sides, but more complexity does seem to move toward upholding the Bible.

A fair conclusion might be to keep digging for the truth, as God seems to want us to do in this faith-based system He's set up. As Dr. Hugh Ross keeps saying, let's look at the evidence as it comes along and track the general direction. Let's see what we learn in the months and years ahead. More questions will always present themselves, something true of science in general, not just evolution.

Darwin himself admitted two rather important problems with his own premise. He asked why there wasn't evidence all over the world proving intermediate forms of life, gradually changing from one species to the next, and why the fossil record presents a sudden (in geological terms) appearance of biological groups. Good questions!

Now that it's been more than one hundred and sixty years since his publication, has the fossil record strengthened or weakened Darwin's theory? Although there is evidence that some simple organisms have changed into even more complex ones, there seems to be a lack of substantial "transitional" fossil evidence that would convince many skeptics that macroevolution tells the story of our history. In other words, there is yet to be a clear cut fossil path tracing back to LUCA (last universal common ancestor). As Dr. Fazale Rana from Reasons to Believe says, "...if the evolutionary paradigm is to be considered a valid model, then the fossil record needs to be replete with transitional forms documenting the actual transformation of one taxon (group of organisms) into another."

In the history of this planet, we call the Cambrian Explosion an explosion because life "exploded!" Fully formed life appeared everywhere, dating back to when God was having lots of fun creating a vast variety of plants and then animals. I picture God creating one thing then another, presents we'd both need and enjoy in the future. Like a Father preparing gifts to put under the Christmas tree, God anticipated our enjoyment one day as we learn about all of the steps He took to allow life on this wonderful planet.

So, why *do* we see fossil records of well-defined, separate species instead of the chaos of gradually mutating creatures? Why not promising "fossil in-betweens," one step leading to the next in the formation of modern man and animals? After all, if the fossil records prove dinosaurs and dodo birds once lived, why can't we find a precise fossil record explaining the Cambrian period?

In their (free!) booklet *What Darwin Didn't Know*, Dr. Fazale Rana and Dr. Hugh Ross from Reasons To Believe tell us one of Darwin's ideas, written to a colleague, was that a prebiotic "soup" created the conditions for all the right chemicals to collide, resulting in the origin of life. Science will strengthen or weaken this hypothesis as newer discoveries are made. For instance, Earth's oldest rocks don't contain the chemicals needed for a prebiotic soup and the planet was inhospitable to life for millions of years. After seven decades of scientists unsuccessfully trying to recreate conditions of this "soup," some are now looking beyond Earth for answers that fit a naturalistic explanation.

Evolution needs time, and lots of it, to entertain the idea that life evolved from very simple forms to the complexities we see today (thinking of the human eye, for example). But Earth's history doesn't allow the time required for such extensive evolution, and as we'll see in a moment, very simple life wasn't so simple, after all.

Since the Universe isn't the static and eternal place first assumed by early scientists (you know, the ones who thought they knew it all), we now know the Universe *isn't* static. There is a finite amount of time in history because there was a beginning. Einstein didn't want this to be the case, he wanted to stick with the eternal timeline which didn't necessarily leave room for divine intervention. But try though he did, Einstein had to admit his famous General Relativity equation was right to confirm earlier suspicions about an expanding Universe.

If our Universe is growing, it had to start somewhere. That means our Universe hasn't been here forever, with limitless time for one lucky accident among nearly infinite tries to create life. As stated in the Preface, limitless time does not explain the *uncaused first cause*: how did any of the elements needed for that accident create themselves out of nothing?

God, as the Creator, didn't have a beginning because He created time along with everything else. He's the uncaused first cause, eternal in a way our human, time-bound brains can't really fathom.

A hostile beginning

We know the beginning of our planet wasn't a friendly place. Like the Universe, it started out hot. Earth was likely a molten planet with lots of exterior dangers (such as meteors that kept on coming during especially unsteady cosmic periods, just ask any dinosaur). Even after the first forms of life appeared, Earth sustained thousands of collisions, some that vaporized oceans, and it took millions of years to heal.

To make matters harder for evolutionists, the first life cells weren't as simple as Darwin would have liked. I won't pretend I know what protoplasm and complex heterogeneous systems are (thank goodness for automatic spell check!) but suffice it to say the earliest fossil organisms which included things like protoplasm and heterogeneous systems were too complex to appear without the helping hand of a creative God. God is that patient Father, letting all of these supernatural steps follow one after another, lovingly anticipating His most complex creature of all: us. We're learning that without all the steps it took to get here, we wouldn't be here at all.

Scientists have long compared biological systems to human-made designs, like motors or machines, with all the parts complementing one another, working together.

Here's a quote from *What Darwin Didn't Know* by Dr. Fazale Rana and Dr. Hugh Ross:

In his 1802 work, <u>Natural Theology</u>, William Paley surveyed a range of biological systems, highlighting their similarities to human-made designs. Human designs are contrivances—things produced with skill and cleverness—and they come about via the work of human agents. Thus, Paley argued, because biological systems are contrivances, they, too, must come about via the work of a Creator.

...neither Paley nor Darwin had any idea of the true complexity and elegance of cellular chemistry and the remarkable similarity between the human-made systems, objects, and devices and the structure and operation of biochemical systems—similarities that vindicate Paley's argument.

For more on William Paley just Google his name along with the "watch analogy" which famously likens the chances of the complexities of life happening by accident to finding a fully functional watch, the pieces having simply fallen into place all by themselves.

About our Sun

It really is a marvel. Darwin thought the sun was a constant energy source ever since the beginning of Earth's history, so he largely ignored that as any sort of big influence on evolution. I won't go into specifics because it involves things like 99% of the Sun's energy coming from nuclear fusion of hydrogen into helium and 1% of nuclear fusion from helium into carbon, nitrogen and oxygen. I have no idea what I just typed, but from what I can glean out of Rana and Ross's book, because of that 1% being different from the 99, the Sun is burning ever more efficiently the older it gets. So today, the sun is between 19 and 24% more luminous than it was at Earth's origin, 4.5 billion years ago. (Maybe that's why we haven't had any more Ice Ages, thank you very much.)

If that luminosity were to change by just 2 percent, life on Earth would end—either by freezing all of the surface water or evaporating all of it. Even a 1 percent change would kill off advanced plants and animals. God has had to make sure it's all balanced and timed so as the Sun increases in brightness, the quantity of greenhouse gases decreased, and our own reflectivity changed enough to maintain the best temperature for life to continue. Over the many years of our planet's existence, God has balanced a lot of "just-rights:" He has had to remove certain life-forms via mass extinctions followed by mass speciation events—those mass extinctions followed by mass replenishments (which fossil records show occurred about every 30 to 35 million years). One benefit from all of these extinctions is the fossil fuel industry, needed to cheaply power modern society.

The miracle of DNA coding

We've known since Dr. Collins mapped the human DNA structure that our cells are made up of four bases: A, T, G, and C. Bases are the building blocks of DNA, and their order and pairing convey information that's unique to every single one of us. I know almost nothing about this, except that when our son was diagnosed with Fragile X Syndrome, we were told that his X chromosome had an excessive repeat of Cs and Gs, resulting in his infirmity. Just one tiny error was a catastrophe for his otherwise healthy brain.

That's basically how scientists realized all the patterns found in DNA was a code: if it didn't follow the right sequence and placement, it breaks down. As Dr. John Carson Lennox says, there is a linguistic element to DNA. Each rung is following an order, and if it's out of that order, it falls apart, just as it did for my son's brain function.

Get this: a coding system of these four bases is found in *every* cell. Think of the structure as rungs of a (twisting) ladder, each rung containing a pair of these four letters. The coding of those letter combinations is over *three billion* rungs long! That's a B, folks, in every single cell. I'd increase the length of this book if I spelled it out. Is the coding in our human DNA an accident, or was it designed by an intelligent designer? We have no known mechanism revealing how RNA and DNA originated.

The complexity of DNA takes far more design than could simply fall into place by random selection, building on earliest life forms. Even Bill Gates has compared DNA to computer codes, only the DNA codes, he said, are far more advanced! A code demands a Coder, because, like computer codes, DNA codes couldn't have written themselves. For a great, easy to watch YouTube video on this subject, check out *The Information Codes Inside Your Body (Long Story Short, Ep. 10)* from Discovery Science. It talks about how the coding in our DNA contains all the information our body needs to grow hair, make blood, muscles, energy production, all the programs of life.

On the DNA proofs
From his website Evolution2.0, Perry Marshall poses some interesting possibilities about the complicated coding process discovered in human DNA. I'm quoting here from his website:
Either:

1. Humans designed DNA
2. Aliens designed DNA
3. DNA occurred randomly and spontaneously
4. There must be some undiscovered law of physics that creates information
5. DNA was Designed by a Superintelligence, i.e. God.

Conclusions:

1. Requires time travel or infinite generations of humans.
2. Could well be true but only pushes the question back in time.

3. May be a remote possibility, but it's not a scientific explanation in that it doesn't refer to a systematic, repeatable process. It's nothing more than an appeal to *luck*.
4. Could be true but no one can form a testable hypothesis until someone observes a naturally occurring code.
5. So the only systematic explanation that remains is (5), a theological one.

To the extent that scientific reasoning can prove anything, DNA is proof of a designer.

Dr. James Tour also asks a challenging question: if we can't recreate DNA with all our intelligent manipulation, how did this occur randomly? The origin of life may still be a mystery in the secular scientific field, but at this point the simplest life forms are known to be anything but simple. He compares the exquisite information (or coding) in early life to the molecules needed in the right state and quantity to be like comparing the difference between the Library of Congress and a box of alphabetic letters. The library has tremendous information while the box of random letters doesn't. Origin of life even in its simplest form requires a great deal of "coding," which points to God.

On the Mind

Besides asking *What is the origin of life?* we should also ask *What is the origin of thought?* Thoughts occur in our mind, but the mind isn't physical matter. It's closer to our soul than our body.

Even Darwin, in an incredibly honest moment of doubt, said if his experiment is correct, how do you account for the evolution of thought? I might add, of rationality? A mindless, unguided process of strict, material evolution doesn't account for why we have a conscience, a mind, the ability to think, or even free will.

Famous physicist Richard Feynman wrote "What affirms our best understanding of reality":

I wonder why. I wonder why.
I wonder why I wonder.
I wonder why I wonder why.
I wonder why I wonder!

While our minds can cause something physical/material to happen (we have an idea and we act on it, or someone else does) the human mind itself can't produce anything. It's not a material thing that evolved from one form to its current, non-material entity. Only the Mind of God as outside of all material things, created us in His image—with a mind capable of love, worship, art, greater learning, planning, even to do math (well, some people have the ability to do math. I do not. Some people like my husband find doing pages of math equations both challenging and relaxing. Go figure.)

On mathematics

Mathematician John Carson Lennox speaks eloquently about how the Apostle John referenced God as "Word," (John 1:1 & 14), linking that to the Genesis account where God repeatedly "said" something on each step of Creation. Today we know the longest word in existence is 3.4 billion letters long, the human genome we talked about in God's coding language right inside our bodies.

Obviously, language is a basic part of Creation, and that language is mathematics.

Sadly, the beauty of math is wasted on people like me, however I'm hoping to understand it better in heaven. At the very least, I'll have an eternity to figure it out. The reason I'd like to understand it, though, is because math is the language of the Universe. How did man figure out how to go to the moon? See the movie *Hidden Figures* and you'll know it was because they learned the already existing laws God put into place, translated through numbers. The laws of the Universe are laws from a Law Giver, who set those mathematical laws into place. In other words, we didn't invent math, we only discovered it.

The fact that mathematics works, and we were able to discover this trustworthy constant, is nothing short of a miracle.

Back to Darwin

In his day, Darwin believed more paleontology evidence would provide the missing transitional forms of life. We just haven't found the right fossils yet, or the transitional forms weren't correctly preserved for us to have found them.

As we discovered in the Archeology section, that particular form of science has only increased since Darwin's era. Paleontology is the same; the study of fossil finds do prove some ancient life is different from life today, and some simpler life preceded complex life. Overall, however, fossil records uncovered today look mostly the same as in Darwin's day. New biological *groups* appeared suddenly, and if there has been any change, it's minimal compared to the vast differences between species. When some truly unique life form appeared, it showed up explosively: from complex cells to animal bodies (hello, Cambrian!).

But the Cambrian explosion had a predecessor. Have you ever heard of the Avalon explosion? Rana and Ross describe that as happening 575 million years ago, when "Ediacaron" life-forms suddenly appeared (I get no help from my spellchecker for Ediacaron, but evidently these are extinct marine organisms from the era we're talking about, being Precambrian). The life-forms discovered from this time were sponges and jellyfish and some other organisms.

This Avalon era coincided with a sudden increase in oxygen in our atmosphere, from 1 to 8 percent. Remember, early Earth was really hostile. Not even enough oxygen! These marine organisms declined about 36 million years later. Scientists still don't know why, but the petroleum companies today are grateful God created so many marine animals.

But that led to the much more impressive Cambrian explosion, some say less than 410,000 years later. Somewhere between 50 and 80 percent of all animal life appeared, and are at least similar to the animals on Earth today. Pretty impressive, particularly since these suddenly appearing animals have little to no connection to the simpler organisms from the Ediacaron life. So instead of relatively simple things originating prior to the Cambrian era then evolving into more complex ones, the fossil records show animals appear independently, early and suddenly.

And guess what? Remember I mentioned the last, mini explosion occurred when oxygen in the Earth's atmosphere went from 1 percent to 8? Well, these more complex creatures couldn't live without 10 percent oxygen in the atmosphere. And that just happens to be when our atmosphere went from 8 to 10 percent oxygen. Oxygen in our atmosphere has fluctuated until roughly 600 million years ago when it grew to about 21% and stabilized. Isn't it amazing that God left so much evidence of the balance required for life? And isn't it amazing that scientists can now understand something that happened so long ago?

Here's another head-scratcher for devotees of evolution. Why, after asteroids and comet strikes, exploding supernovas, gamma-ray bursts and super volcano eruptions, were there so many exterminations (40 to 90 percent of life forms), and then, once Earth stabilized, new life forms appeared? (Look up the 5 Big Extinctions, two of which wiped out the dinosaurs.) Why did life forms return so rapidly, with even better adaptations to their contemporaneous ecology?

Without God continuing creation throughout the long fifth and sixth days, these replenishments on Earth are a definite challenge for scientists to explain. But it's all in the Bible. Read Psalm 104 as a reflection of creation events and see if verse 30 stands out as it did for me. It says He "renews the face of the earth." This is God replacing what was needed after Earth suffered losses when its environment was still hostile.

On those transition forms

In Rana and Ross's pamphlet, they explain three transitional fossils that evolutionists claim as proof of Darwin's theory. My favorite is the feathered dinosaur leading to birds, it just sounds so cute. Problem? There were still feathered dinosaurs *after* birds came into the picture. So how did they evolve from one species into the other, if they were co-existing, independent creatures? Did one branch evolve while the other remained the same? Why do more primitive fossils of feathered dinosaurs still appear after birds came on the scene?

Two other challenges are "fishapods" into tetrapods and raccoon-like creatures into whales (fishapods potentially dwelling on both sea and land that changed into the first land-dwelling vertebrates). The fossil records don't reveal a linear evolution with gradual changes over time as evolution would demand for either of these instances. Rather, all these animals coexisted, overlapping each other. Confusing this further, more primitive forms of fishapods show up after more advanced forms, so they evidently have a complicated history known only to God at this point.

The evolution connection between the two is not simple. Leaving land for water in one case and the opposite for the other would mean adapting anatomically and physiologically from one environment to the other. Even geologists who believe this to be the case describe these major changes as "rapid". Ten million years may sound like a long time to you and to me, but on an earth that is probably 4.5 billion years old, that's like the snap of a finger, especially for such a vast change to their makeup.

The evolutionary process was assumed to be not only unpredictable but also non-repeatable, because of the accidental, non-directed nature of the theory. However, Rana has offered more than one hundred examples of convergence, or repeated, biochemical systems—evolution repeating itself, when the nature of evolution would expect the opposite. Could a better explanation be that God used a successful template more than once, just as any efficient inventor would? Why is our DNA so similar to apes? Or bananas, for that matter, since about half of our genetic makeup is similar to my husband's favorite fruit. It's because God is the ultimate Engineer, and He knows how to be efficient.

On the evolution of man

Darwin claimed that because we closely compare anatomically and embryologically with apes, we must have descended from LUCA. No God needed.

Scientists have uncovered the remains of species that evolutionists like to think are our common ancestors: Hominids, Homo Erectus, and Neanderthals (among a few others), or at least close branches from the same original tree. Records show these living beings were fairly intelligent, at least enough to use some crude tools (some animals do that) and gather together in what can be called a "culture" (even pack animals do that) and even cook some of their food. But Hugh Ross has a convincing argument that since these creatures did not possess any understanding of symbolism (included in that would be any form of worship, art, ornamentation, even language) they were not made in the image of God (and thus had no soul). Plus, their "technology" (use of crude tools and their limited culture similar to apes) remained the same throughout their entire appearance on Earth, despite being here longer than us (first fossils date back between 250,000 to 200,000 years ago, and disappeared around 40,000 years ago). Unlike mankind, they didn't progress spiritually, culturally, or technologically. Since we're made in the image of God, and they weren't, it's not surprising they didn't have the benefits that come with being exceptionally different from the animal world.

Wherever these creatures have been found, animal populations remained steady upon the eventual arrival of modern man (descendants of Adam and Eve). Neanderthals and the like were basically forerunners to man, allowing the animal kingdom over which we have reign to stand a chance against extinction. Without creatures like Neanderthals coming before us, animals did not learn to fear upright hunters using tools to kill. They were less likely to hide, therefore easy to hunt until such behaviors were learned.

There is also convincing evidence that Neanderthals didn't descend from a common ancestor to us, simply because of the vast differences between us and them. Investigators recovered maternal DNA from five Neanderthal specimens and learned the mtDNA sequences were too different for us to have descended from them. We now know that man did not descend from Neanderthals, although modern DNA investigation does reveal there was some interbreeding between modern man and Neanderthals. This accounts for Neanderthal DNA being found in modern ancestry tracing. But, like a lion and a tiger interbreeding to make a "Liger" such offspring is called a hybrid, not that one descended from another.

According to Rana and Ross, many scientific studies indicate that humanity originated perhaps as long ago as 100,000 years in or near East Africa. Dating is difficult in this range. A Biblical date for the creation of Adam and Eve would be anywhere between 60,000 to 100,000 years ago. (*Navigating Genesis*, P. 75, by Hugh Ross) Through the study of mitochondrial (mtDNA) and Y-chromosomal DNA markers, scientists can trace the history of human life. mtDNA comes from the mother and the Y from the father. Even with still unanswered questions as to exact dates of origin, the more we learn about genetics and DNA the smaller the original group of humans becomes (we're getting closer to Adam and Eve all the time).

What's the big deal about a Big Bang?

In his book *The Case for A Creator*, Lee Strobel introduces the reader to "the greatest observational cosmologist in the world:" Allan Rex Sandage. Dr. Sandage was an atheist for most of his life. At the beginning of his marriage, he even drew his wife away from her faith. However, after years of study of both science and the Bible, he came to realize there must be a God. According to Strobel's account, Sandage publicly acknowledged his status as a Christian to the surprise of everyone at a 1985 conference on science and religion. Sandage's reputation as an atheist was renowned, but here he proclaimed that at age fifty he'd decided to become a Christian.

What convinced him is hard to pinpoint, but he did say the Big Bang can't be explained within physics except as a supernatural event. It was only through faith in a Creator that he could resolve the mysteries of science.

Attending that conference was Stephen Meyer. He is a former geophysicist and professor with degrees in both physics and geology, and masters in history and philosophy from Cambridge. His doctorate is also from Cambridge, in origin-of-life biology. He now directs the Discovery Institute's Center for Science and Culture. Hearing Sandage speak was the first time Dr. Meyer considered how science could provide evidence for his Christian faith. Since then he has been an avid supporter of the Intelligent Design movement.

In Strobel's interview with him, Dr. Meyer harkened back to a quote from Galileo: "Science tells you how the heavens go, and the Bible tells you how to go to heaven." In other words, although some say science only needs to explain what elements exist, the nature of gravity, etc. the Bible explains *why* it all started: from a loving Creator making a way for mankind to freely accept Him and ultimately to share eternity.

Cosmology textbooks credit Penzias and Wilson with the discovery of the cosmic microwave background (leftover energy from the Big Bang). This established the Big Bang theory of cosmology, proving that the Universe was born at a definite moment. This was back in 1964, after a fellow named George Gamow, in 1946, had figured there must be a reason Earth has all the elements we need to sustain life. Only an expanding Universe that started from an unbelievably hot beginning could account for these elements existing throughout the Universe. Edwin Hubble, in 1929, had already confirmed the Universe was indeed expanding, because he observed light from distant galaxies from all over the sky appears more red than what would be expected. He figured out the "red shift" was due to those galaxies moving away from us: i.e. support for an expanding Universe.

But it was actually a Jesuit priest by the name of Abbé Georges Lemaître who, in 1925, was among the first to promote the idea of a single point for the beginning of the Universe. Atheistic astronomer Fred Hoyle made fun of the new idea by calling it a Big Bang. The name stuck—we do love our alliteration, don't we? By the end of Fred Hoyle's life, however, he believed life as we know it "must have been the result of some unseen intelligence" and that "there is a coherent plan for the Universe, although I have no idea what it is."

All of this was on the shoulders of Albert Einstein who published his General Relativity theory in 1916 after years of work. He'd really wanted to go with the so-called wisdom of the day that believed everything was static, unchanging and eternal, but had to admit trying to step away from what he knew to be true about the Universe expanding was the greatest blunder of his career.

If only all these scientists had read the Old Testament. I'm sure the good Abbé did. According to Hugh Ross in his book *The Creator and the Cosmos*, the science of a Big Bang was already written in the Bible, where it states there was nothing and then there was something. God began creation *ex nihilo* or "out of nothing." Scripture says that which we see today was made from what couldn't be seen before: something out of nothing. (Heb. 11:3)

If the Universe had a beginning, it couldn't be eternal. Because it originated from one place, it must have expanded from that one place. Those are the two simple ingredients needed for a "bang": *something from nothing, and an expansion from a single spot.*

Maybe it's the "bang" Christians don't like, suggesting everything around us exploded due to a random, natural process. Maybe it's simply that people automatically but unnecessarily connect the Big Bang theory to evolution, or a beginning without the necessity of God. After all, public schoolrooms leave no room to consider a Designer. Separation of church and state and all that.

There's absolutely nothing random about Earth's history, because God has always, from the first step of creation until today and into eternity, had His Hand on creation. To quote Dr. Ross, our Universe is so well designed for the cosmic expansion scientists have observed that it's one more factor proving the improbability that any of this happened by accident. For the Universe to provide and protect a planet Earth suitable for any kind of life, there must be a perfect balance of mass density and space-energy density. I don't actually know what such terms mean (something to do with how many particles something has in relation to how much space it takes up) but here's my point: Mass density fine-tuning is better than 1 part in 10 to the 60th power—that's one chance in a 1 with 60 zeroes after it. If you think that's a teeny-tiny chance, the space-energy density is twice as impressive: 1 part in 10 to the 120th power (120 zeroes after that 1).

If you have something hot that expands, it stands to reason that it will also be cooling. That's another ingredient necessary to the Big Bang theory. Cooling.

What does the Bible say about an expanding Universe, the idea that spurred the Big Bang theory? In words written 2,500 years ago, Isaiah claims God created the heavens (the cosmos) and stretched them out. (Isaiah 40:22 and 44:24) There are multiple verses using this same term about the heavens being stretched, in fact eleven times, not only from Isaiah but from Job, Psalms, Jeremiah and Zechariah.

There are plenty of verses in the Bible that state God alone created everything and that God is in the process, even today, of letting it "stretch." (Psalm 104:2, Jeremiah 10:12 and 51:15) He simultaneously laid out creation and finished making all the laws, constants and equations that describe creation, while allowing the "stretching out" to continue to this day. It's "complete" yet "ongoing." A mystery to understand, a miracle of a description considering it was written so long ago. In Calvin's Commentary of Jeremiah 33:25, he states God fixed the laws of nature which remain unchangeable.

Knowing that science confirms rather than denies the Word of God is a huge faith-builder for me.

• • •

What about the Cultural Big Bang?

One of the many reasons I've enjoyed putting this book together is exploring things I'd never heard about before. A cultural Big Bang is one of them. About 40,000 to 45,000 years ago, fossil records show a boom in agriculture, in cities, in symbolism and art and jewelry and language. Some jewelry beads and decorated ostrich eggs date even farther back than this, between 60,000 and 80,000 years ago. According to the Smithsonian Magazine, there is evidence for wild grain consumption taken from residue on tools dating 105,000 years ago. As archeology continues, there will likely be more precise dating for the earliest human cultures.

All these dates are within the range of when God created Adam and Eve, allowing time for humans to have multiplied as God instructed, then migrate from Eden along routes that existed during the last big Ice Age. The location of four rivers meeting in the Garden described in Genesis narrows the spot for Eden, namely: the Euphrates, Tigris, Pishon and Gihon. (Genesis 2:10-14) The Euphrates and Tigris still exist; the Gihon river is thought by many to be the Karun River running through Iraq. The Pishon, the Bible says, traverses Havilah. According to archeologist Joel P. Kramer, Havilah is Saudi Arabia, based on Genesis 25:18 as being east of Egypt in the direction of Assyria. There is also gold and onyx found there, along with aromatic resins traded along Arabia's "incense route." Smooth pebbles of black basalt, quartz and granite originating from the Hijaz mountains are still found in dry river beds running hundreds of miles toward where the Tigris, Euphrates and Gihon join as one. Evidence of this ancient river was first spotted by satellite and is called the Wadi Ar Rumah. It could be that Eden is beneath the marshy land of southern Iraq at the northern tip of the Persian Gulf. This area would have been above sea level at this time, and warm enough to sustain life even during an Ice Age. This was anywhere from 13,000 to 130,000 years ago.

Evolutionists don't really know why "early man" suddenly

turned into modern man, and this date could be adjusted in the future as the dating measure for this time period becomes more precise. The fact is, culture erupted rather quickly and consistently around the world. Was it because of a mutation that was so successful they easily dominated any other branch of evolutionary "man?" My personal experience with mutations is too negative to believe this, since Fragile X Syndrome is a mutation. Mutations don't tend to make something better!

It's generally accepted we didn't evolve from Neanderthals, even in secular circles, but at least one scientist I read about suggested if a genetic glitch happened in the Neanderthal line the way it happened in whatever form of early man it did happen in, we'd have descended from Neanderthals instead. It was all just a glitch in one form of early (Cro-Magnon) man, and here we are.

Personally, I think faith in a "glitch" is harder to come by than faith in the God of our Bible.

What's the big deal about fine-tuning?

We'll start with the **cosmological constant.** What in the world is that? Or should I say what in the Universe is that? Well, here's an answer that will be as clear as mud for the non-scientist readers like me: it's the energy density of empty space. Need more? How about this: it has to do with the gravity and anti-gravity of an expanding Universe. Glad we got that cleared up!

Actually, I wanted to stick with this even though it's hard to understand because Hugh Ross says it's something so amazing this fact alone is profound evidence of divine design.

Evidently this factor is part of Einstein's equation for General Relativity. That's enough for me to give up real understanding, but when Einstein first proposed the idea of a cosmological constant, he was ridiculed for it (who knew there was so much ridicule in science?). Anyway, he predicted that space (regardless of matter associated with it) would stretch itself out, and the more it stretched, the faster it would stretch.

Back in 1998, scientists observed a giant exploding star that confirmed the "constant" speeds up the expansion while the "mass" of the Universe slows the expansion because of gravity. When our Universe was younger, gravity was King. But now that the Universe is elegantly aged and getting larger (I ask you, who doesn't get larger with age?) the cosmological constant has superseded gravity's effect.

Any difference in the mass (the braking effect due to gravity) or in the cosmological constant (the stretching effect of energy) and we wouldn't have the just-right living conditions we now enjoy. In fact, we wouldn't be here at all. Suffice it to say the probability of fine-tuning for this detail is one chance in a 1 with lots and lots of zeroes after it (try 120).

Scientists would expect this constant to be very large but is, in fact, small enough to be perfect for us.

In their book *I Don't Have Enough Faith to be an Atheist*, Norman Geisler and Frank Turek refer to the Teleological Argument:

1. Every design had a designer.
2. The Universe has a highly complex design.
3. Therefore, the Universe had a designer.

Makes sense to me. It goes along with William Lane Craig's Kalam Cosmological Argument:

1. Everything that begins to exist has a cause.
2. The Universe began to exist.
3. Therefore the Universe has a cause.

Atheists argue nothing that's material can be made from something that's non-material, but who can put a limit to God?

Also from the Geisler/Turek book, based on the absolutely inhospitable beginning of our planet, coupled with how inhospitable the Universe is, we live in a remarkably stable time. Here are a few constants (or "fixed" as Scripture says, meaning dependably stable) for life to survive here on Earth:

- **Precise atmospheric composition** including exact levels of nitrogen, oxygen, carbon dioxide, and ozone. Remember I mentioned how the oxygen level fluctuated during the Avalon and then the Cambrian explosions? Well, the oxygen level has been stable for about 600 million years. Carbon dioxide levels too high and we'd burn up. If it were lower, our plants would die and then so would we.
- **Atmospheric Transparency.** This means the sunlight has to penetrate our atmosphere, but not *too* much or we'd get radiation poisoning.
- **Moon-earth gravitational interaction.** If gravity between us and the moon were any greater, the gravitational pull would change the tidal effects on our oceans, atmosphere and the rotation of our planet. If it were any less, orbital changes would cause disastrous climate instabilities. Either way, we wouldn't be here at all.
- **Overall gravity.** If our gravitational force was changed by 0.0000000000000000000000000000000000001 percent our sun wouldn't exist and neither would we. That's 37 zeroes after that decimal point!
- Precisely balanced **planetary movement.**
- **Water vapor levels** too great would lead to runaway greenhouse problems and temps would rise too high for us to survive. Any less and we wouldn't have enough greenhouse effect and it would be too cold for us to live.
- My favorite planet, after Earth, is **Jupiter**. Between its size and gravitational pull it's like a cosmic "vacuum cleaner," attracting things that would otherwise spell disaster for us: too many asteroids and comets. Jupiter is our shield. Yay for Jupiter!

- The **Earth's crust** is "just right" as Goldilocks would say. Any thicker and there would be too much oxygen transferred up through a deeper, more involved root system in the crust (oxygen is produced via the plants) and a thinner, more delicate crust would leave us open to volcanoes and earthquakes too frequent to allow us life.
- The **Earth's rotation** is also "just right." If it took longer than twenty-four hours, temperatures would vary too much between night and day. Any shorter and atmospheric wind velocities would blow us away.
- If our 23 degree **axial tilt** were altered even a bit, surface temps would become too extreme.
- If our **lightning** rate were greater, there would be disastrous fire consequences; too little and there goes some of the nitrogen we need to fix the soil so we can eat. We need lightning for the Earth-atmosphere electrical balance.
- More **earthquakes** would threaten more human life, but if we had no earthquakes, nutrients from erosion carried to the sea via river runoff and ending up on the ocean floor wouldn't cycle back to the continents.
- If the **stars** were any closer or farther apart, planetary orbits would be affected. That's why the Universe is as big as it is. David says it best in Psalm 19: The heavens declare the glory of God!

I've only listed most of those that I found in the Geisler/Turek book, but Hugh Ross has said that for all of the 122 constants to come together by chance so that we could live in this stable environment, the probability would be our planet in the number of existing planets we know (conservatively) being 10 to the 22 power (a 1 followed by 22 zeroes). For that one planet among so many to possess all of the characteristics we need to sustain life, those 122 constants, would be one in 10 with 138 zeroes after it. I won't waste the paper or ink to convince you this is an unimaginably precise number, meaning the chances of our planet providing the just right conditions for life at the just right moment in cosmic history is a miracle.

Hold on, though! Maybe there are so many Universes out there, an infinite number, so that one of them finally, finally, got it right. That replaces the infinite time to get it right that Einstein eliminated with an infinity of a different kind.

Right now, there is no evidence for multiple Universes. So, you say, we just don't have the technology to find them! Like Darwin, those who are looking for multiple Universes have faith the future will vindicate their belief system.

But it's hard to imagine an infinite number of anything that's actually material and not have *some* clue of anything infinite going on.

Or even if there aren't actual "alien" civilizations sent here to be fruitful and multiply, maybe conditions out there in space came together via either drifting or comets carrying them to and fro enough times for the lucky accident of life to happen. You'd still need a creation event for these mysterious pieces to exist in the first place, no matter how lucky their journey.

Either way, if such a thing as "panspermia" exists or there are multiple Universes, then what either one of these rather far-fetched ideas do is demand a need for a Designer there, too. Another Big Bang with all the right pieces falling into place for survival in a hostile environment or exist at all takes the same kind of "infinite" belief I have in an infinite God. What does panspermia or an unobservable, unseen multiple Universe theory demand except faith in an even bigger design?

It appears every belief system requires some amount of faith.

In a recent lecture Hugh Ross gave regarding fine-tuning, he presented a sequence of things that needed to be just right for our Earth to sustain life as we know it. Each piece is connected to the next with exquisite balance. First you need:

- A **Universe**, and within that Universe:
- A **supergalaxy cluster** like ours, which have all the right features needed for life, and within that:
- A **galaxy cluster** and group, with just right spiral and symmetrical arms, and within that:
- A **galaxy** orbiting a just right star (our sun):
- A **sun** with just right stability and luminosity (Astronomers sometimes encounter twin stars but they have yet to discover one that's remotely similar to our sun. The closest look-alike is 5,000 times inferior to ours.)
- Jupiter, Saturn, Venus and the rest of our **solar system planets**. We've observed about 5,000 planets orbiting different stars and none of them do the job our solar system does to *support and protect* any specific planet within their system.
- **Earth**
- **Moon**, just the right size and distance (though it's bigger than other moons orbiting other planets). The current scientific model for moon formation is that a huge, Mars-sized object hit Earth at just the right spot, causing debris to break off from Earth but not obliterate it. The object and the debris coalesced as our moon. Even the size of the impact had to be perfect: not too big or it would destroy Earth, too little and the debris would've dissipated too quickly for the moon to form. As already mentioned, the moon's gravitational pull slows our rotation to twenty-four-hour days and steadies our tilt. Without the moon we wouldn't have a stable climate, and altered ocean tides would screw up our coastal ecosystems.

No other planet is like ours, or like any of the planets in our solar system. I don't believe luck explains it. If the planets in our solar system weren't exactly as they are we wouldn't be here. That includes our comet and asteroid belts. Eighty percent of other stars have these belts, but only ours is just right.

———

Stated as simply as possible, it comes down to this: Did we get here by chance? Is the history of our Universe solely materialistic? I just can't answer Yes based on these points:

1. Origins: the Universe and its laws, life, morality, mind, spirit.
2. Existence: Evil, sin, suffering, beauty, humor, love and Truth.
3. The Universe has extraordinary, miraculous fine-tuning.
4. DNA contains information that forms a code.

This section is probably the hardest for me to understand in much depth, but easy enough to see the incredible involvement God has had, and continues to have, with our planet. I know this isn't the Prophecy section, and this is just my opinion, but the fact that we can now verify scientifically what God did so long ago suggests to me that God is revealing Himself in a new way. I won't repeat Lord Kelvin's mistake and say science knows all it's ever going to know, but I do believe science has revealed God's meticulous Hand so convincingly that in some ways it only takes common sense to see God's existence. Perhaps this is God's way of bringing more people to Him before history comes to an end.

In any case, the incredible account of creation as written in the Bible makes me want to sing along with Mercy Me: "...how could I not worship You?"

Wisdom and the Human Experience

I've recruited my older (and wiser) brother, Pastor Mark Gilbert, to contribute this important chapter. Mark introduced me to the gospel when I was a kid, and has been among my favorite "go-to" resources ever since.

By Mark Gilbert, M.Div

Intro – It seems that our human experience, life on this marvelous planet, has become somewhat more confusing in recent years. Some leading contributors to our confusion have been technology, politics and rapidly changing social mores. I won't go into the details of this confusion here but all one has to do to get a glimpse of our world's confusion and disorientation is watch one of the many 24/7 news channels now available. So, is there anywhere we can turn to discover wisdom that will make sense of our human experience? This book has already set forth that source; it's the Bible. The Bible presents a wisdom that clarifies our confusion and makes sense of our human experience if we are willing to listen. What follows is only a small taste of that wisdom.

. . .

What is Wisdom?

Where does wisdom come from? How should we define wisdom? What makes someone wise? Is it education, a beautiful mind, common sense? We live in a world that is more educated and technically advanced than it has ever been. Yet we live in a world that in the past century has seen more death and destruction from man's inhumanity to man than in its entire prior history. So it seems that education and advancements in technology don't automatically lead to a world full of wisdom. I ask again: What is wisdom?

This book asks the question: why should we believe? One reason we should believe is because God has revealed His wisdom to us in his Word. Wisdom is a gift from God. Here's what Paul writes to the Christians in Colossae:

> For this reason, since the day we heard about you, we have not stopped praying for you. We continually **ask** God to fill you with the knowledge of his will through all the **wisdom** and understanding that the Spirit gives. (Colossians 1:9 NIV)

Wisdom is a gift of God's Spirit that is intimately connected to God's truth, God's knowledge. I like simple, short definitions of complicated ideas whenever possible. With that in mind I would define wisdom as *the application of God's truth to life in the power of the Holy Spirit*. If we want to be truly wise, we need to know and understand the truth God has revealed to us, apply it to the circumstances of life as we trust in the leading of God's Spirit. So, what does God's wisdom tell us about our human experience?

Wisdom and Why We Are

It always seems wise to begin at the beginning. In the Book of Genesis God clearly tells us who we are and why we are here:

> [26]Then God said, *Let us make mankind in our image, in our likeness, so that they may rule over the fish in the sea and the birds in*

the sky, over the livestock and all the wild animals, and over all the creatures that move along the ground.

[27]*So God created mankind in his own image, in the image of God he created them; male and female he created them.*

[28]*God blessed them and said to them, Be fruitful and increase in number; fill the earth and subdue it. Rule over the fish in the sea and the birds in the sky and over every living creature that moves on the ground.* (Genesis 1:26-28 NIV)

In these verses God reveals several things about who we are and why we are here. In so doing he begins to reveal our meaning and purpose. He tells us that we are created in his image. In fact, we are the only thing created in God's image. Our likeness to God is not physical but functional and essential. We are like God in what we do, how we do it and in the essence of our being.

Amazingly, God tells us that we are created to rule; and ruling is a God activity. Ruling the spiritual and physical reality is something God does! Yet at the very dawn of our existence, we are charged by God himself with ruling this world! As rulers created in God's likeness, we are to rule in a way that reflects that likeness. As Adam and Eve walked with God, they would have learned what that meant. They would have grown spiritually, socially and intellectually so as to fulfill their God given role properly.

We are also told we were created male and female which is the foundation for human relationship. It reflects the fact that God as a triune being, Father, Son and Holy Spirit is essentially a relational, social being. In the creation story there is only one thing that was not good; that was when man was alone before God created the woman. So we too are relational beings created to interact and socialize with others of our kind and with our creator.

We are remarkable beings. But as wonderful as we are, we remain physical, limited beings. Try as we might we are not God. We have needs, needs that were to be met in our relationship with God, in the management of this world and in the abundance of the garden. Larry Crab in his book *In Side Out* makes the case that all human beings have two essential desires that we spend our life trying to fulfill. We will see why these desires have become needs in a moment, but these desires are for *security* and *significance*. Security is the desire to know that we are loved unconditionally and if possible, perfectly by another. We want to find a sense of security and rest in the knowledge and experience of this loving relationship. Significance is the desire to know that our life has meaning beyond ourself, that our life impacts others in a positive, meaningful way.

As we look at the creation account, we see that God met these desires perfectly for us. We find our significance in ruling over this world. We were given the privilege of managing this world in such a way that the influence of God as seen in the Garden would be spread all around this globe. We would then find significance in spreading God's creative work throughout this world. We were to rule in such a way that the natural beauty and harmony of the garden were spread from the garden to all the earth. At the same time, we were to rule the world so that all the physical needs of an expanding human race were met. Remember we were to be fruitful and fill the earth. So our need for significance, knowing our life has meaning beyond itself and that we positively impact others, was perfectly met in the job we were given to do.

Our security was found in our relationships. We had a perfect, loving relationship with our creator God. This is seen in the gift of the garden, the privilege of sharing in God's activity of ruling, God's fellowship with man in the garden and the gift of male/female relationships. Adam expressed the wonder and wealth of his relationship with Eve in Genesis 2:21-25: (NIV)

> [21]So the Lord God caused the man to fall into a deep sleep; and while he was sleeping, he took one of the man's ribs and then closed up the place with flesh. [22]Then the Lord God made a woman from the rib he had taken out of the man, and he brought her to the man.
>
> [23]The man said,
> *This is now bone of my bones*

and flesh of my flesh;
she shall be called 'woman,'
for she was taken out of man.

[24]That is why a man leaves his father and mother and is united to his wife, and they become one flesh.

[25]Adam and his wife were both naked, and they felt no shame.

These verses clearly indicate that Adam was thrilled about the creation of the woman and saw the priority of this relationship over all other earthly relationships. Both the man and the woman were secure in the relationship they had with God and each other. So everything was good. In fact, God said everything was very good when he had finished creating Adam and Eve. Man and woman found their security in their relationship with God and each other. They found their significance in the job of ruling over this marvelous world under the direction of their loving creator. What could go wrong?

Wisdom and What Went Wrong

As I have said earlier, the world in which we now live is a marvelous place. It has beauty, opportunity, life, growth, fulfillment, love and a host of other good things. But it is also a place of death, decay, disappointment, loss, failure, selfishness, hatred and a host of other evils. So what happened to the very good life in the garden? Somehow evil, something less than good, entered God's good creation.

I am sure that most of us are familiar with the account of man's temptation and fall. I will not get into the philosophical and theological discussions about the origins, meaning and purpose of evil. My intent is more practical. I want to look at the practice of evil and its result in our life. After that we will look at the solution to the evil in this world and our own personal life.

So what went wrong? Well, Eve ate a piece of forbidden fruit and Adam willingly joined her. That was it. The terrible deed that brought all the evil we see in the world today! Do you mean to say that all the tragedies and troubles of this entire world were caused by someone eating a piece of fruit? You've got to be kidding! No, I'm not and yes, I do! Let me explain. Scripture teaches that the highest good is always a tested good. Here is one example of many about this teaching from the Bible:

> [6]So be truly glad. There is wonderful joy ahead, even though you must endure many trials for a little while. [7]These trials will show that your faith is genuine. It is being tested as fire tests and purifies gold—though your faith is far more precious than mere gold. So when your faith remains strong through many trials, it will bring you much praise and glory and honor on the day when Jesus Christ is revealed to the whole world. (1 Peter 1:6-7 NLT)

God allows trials and difficulties in our life to assure us that our faith is genuine. Our trials in life also layup for us treasure in heaven that will result in our praise, glory and honor when Christ returns. So in Genesis, God sets up a test for Adam and Eve to show the genuine nature of their faith and trust in Him. This test will raise their faith to the level of the highest good, a tested and approved good. For Adam and Eve the kind of test was irrelevant. It simply had to be a test of their trust and obedience to God. Would they obey God, trust his warnings about disobedience and its consequences, or would they rebel and follow their own desires regardless of the reason or consequences?

Sadly, they chose to disobey. They failed the test and evil, something less than the good they had been given, was introduced into the world.

The evil is immediately apparent in their lives. The first thing they do is to fashion a camouflage covering in hopes of hiding from God when he comes to them in the garden. Guilt has already poisoned their relationship with God. When God does meet them in the garden and asks if they have eaten from the tree of Good and

Evil they immediately try to avoid their own culpability. Adam accuses his wife of leading him astray. And Eve accuses the Serpent for her failure. Both in their own way accuse God for their failure. Adam says it was this woman *you* gave to be with me who gave me the fruit to eat. And Eve says she was deceived by the serpent who was created by God. Fear, guilt, insecurity, doubt and division have replaced the security, significance and blessings of life in the ideal garden. The result of sin in our life is always two-fold: separation and loss. Separation from God and the loss of his best in our life. Separation from others and the loss of a healthy, wholesome relationship.

As I said earlier my intent is to be practical. How did Eve fail? I think Eve followed the path of all sinful failure. It is a three-step process we all, unfortunately, follow at times. We see this path clearly in Genesis 3:

> [1]The serpent was the shrewdest of all the wild animals the Lord God had made. One day he asked the woman, *Did God really say you must not eat the fruit from any of the trees in the garden?*
>
> [2]*Of course we may eat fruit from the trees in the garden,* the woman replied. [3]*It's only the fruit from the tree in the middle of the garden that we are not allowed to eat. God said, 'You must not eat it or even touch it; if you do, you will die.'*
>
> [4]*You won't die!* the serpent replied to the woman. [5]*God knows that your eyes will be opened as soon as you eat it, and you will be like God, knowing both good and evil.*
>
> [6]The woman was convinced. She saw that the tree was beautiful and its fruit looked delicious, and she wanted the wisdom it would give her. So she took some of the fruit and ate it. Then she gave some to her husband, who was with her, and he ate it, too. [7]At that moment their eyes were opened, and they suddenly felt shame at their nakedness. So they sewed fig leaves together to cover themselves. (Genesis 3:1-7 NLT)

First, she questioned and then ultimately rejected the truth. In

Eve's case the questioning of the truth was prompted by the serpent and his lies: 'Did God say you must not eat...' and again: 'you won't die' when in fact that is exactly what God said. The serpent also says that through their disobedience they will not die but actually become 'like God'.

Eve's questioning of the truth came from the serpent but our questioning of the truth can come from any one of a multitude of sources. Often it's our own inner self that questions God's truth. It might be our circumstances that prompt us to doubt God's truth, or others, or a host of sources in this less-than-perfect world in which we live. But the point is this: we begin down the path of evil when we question and then reject God's truth.

Here are some of the doubts about God's truth we might have:

- Does God really love me?
- Can God really forgive that sin?
- Is God's moral path worth it?
- If everyone does it, can it be that bad?

And we could go on and on.

The second step toward moral failure and evil is to embrace a lie.

We see this clearly in the passage above: *The woman was convinced. She saw that the tree was beautiful and its fruit looked delicious, and she wanted the wisdom it would give her.* Eve had fully embraced a lie that was contrary to God's truth. She would soon discover there was no benefit from embracing a lie, only loss. However, a lie often appears more attractive than the truth and we, like Eve, embrace the lie.

There was one final step left; she needed to act on the lie, which she promptly did: *So she took some of the fruit and ate it. Then she gave some to her husband, who was with her, and he ate it, too.* Their rebellion was complete. They had rejected the truth, embraced a lie, and then willfully acted on the lie rather than the truth. They immediately experienced the consequences of acting on the lie.

Rather than becoming more like God they experienced guilt, shame, separation and loss. How sad!

Big and little evils all have the same source: rebellion against God's truth. A person rejects the truth, embraces a lie and then acts on the lie. Adolf Hitler was a big evil. He rejected the truth that all people are created in God's image and have intrinsic, eternal worth. He then embraced a lie: I can create a super race and a Third Reich that will last a thousand years by eliminating undesirables. He then acted on that lie and brought about the death of millions of Jews, gypsies, homosexuals and the mentally infirm!

But there are little evils that we embrace every day. The truth: *husbands love your wives as Christ loves the church.* A husband can reject that truth by thinking "my wife doesn't deserve my love because she has been so inconsiderate of me lately." God's truth rejected. He then can embrace a lie: "my wife needs to learn a lesson and I'm the one to teach her." A lie embraced! He then acts on that lie: "I will give her the silent treatment for a few days and see how she likes that!" A little evil that may only hurt a few people but still evil with the same miserable spiritual result: separation and loss.

Separation and loss are the sad results of all our sin. When Adam and Eve sinned they were separated from God. The almost comical sewing of fig leaves to cover themselves was, I believe, an attempt to hide from God more than an attempt to cover their physical nakedness. Sin had separated them from their loving creator God, resulting in fear, guilt, shame and separation. They had a deep desire to hide from God. Sin had produced separation.

Sin then produced a mountain of loss in their lives. They lost the security they had in their relationship with God and with each other. It was replaced with fear, guilt, accusations and a host of other ills. They lost the significance of managing a cooperative creation as the ground was cursed and their fruitful management of the creation became labored toil. We see all these unhappy results of sin continuing in our world and in our personal lives to this day! So, is all lost?

. . .

Wisdom and the Conquest of Evil

Fortunately, God was not going to lose this struggle with evil. The serpent would not win. God makes his first promise of victory in Genesis when he says to the serpent:

> "And I will put enmity between you and the woman and between your offspring and hers; he will crush your head, and you will strike his heel." (Genesis 3:15 NIV)

The offspring of the woman would defeat evil. This offspring would be bruised in the process but he would utterly defeat evil as he crushes the head of the serpent. This promise of victory is developed throughout Scripture and finds its fulfillment in the life, death and resurrection of Jesus Christ. Jesus becomes a new Adam, a new perfect representative and test case for all humanity. He was a person tested and tempted in every way we are but without failure, without sin. Listen to Hebrews 4:15 (NIV):

> For we do not have a high priest who is unable to empathize with our weaknesses, but we have one who has been **tempted** in every way, just as we are—yet he did not sin!

Jesus resisted every temptation thrown at him. He passed every kind of test a person can face in this world. His greatest test was far more challenging than the one given to Adam. In fact, it was a test far more challenging than any test we could possibly experience. It was a test that only Jesus could face. As the perfect Son of God, the one who lived a perfect life, he was asked to die in our place, to take our sin and the punishment for that sin on himself even though he deserved none of it. He was asked to experience the separation and loss that was rightly ours. He was asked to experience the ultimate separation and loss which is death itself—for us! The Good News is that he accepted this test, the plan of God to transfer our sin and guilt to his beloved Son and give us his perfect life and righteousness in exchange! Listen to 2 Corinthians 5:21 (NIV):

God made him who had no sin to be sin for us, so that in him we might become the righteousness of God.

This is called grace!

And God has made the way of receiving that grace remarkably simple. God's grace is received by faith. Again, listen to these verses from Ephesians 2:8-9 (NIV):

> [8]For it is by grace you have been saved, through faith—and this is not from yourselves, it is the gift of God— [9]not by works, so that no one can boast.

God has made it incredibly simple to receive his grace, we accept it by faith. But simplicity doesn't mean ease. It seems we humans, ever since sin entered our lives, don't give our trust very easily. Rather than simply give our trust, we want others to earn our trust. We find it even harder to give our trust completely to anyone. We want to hold on to some of our trust and keep it in ourselves. The same is true when we are asked to trust God. I will trust in God but also in my religion, my good works, even my doubts. Look again at Ephesians 2:8-9 above and you will see that we cannot trust in anything that we might want to boast about: religion, good works or anything else. God asks us to trust him completely, to rely solely on him and what he has done for us in Christ. That is a challenge, but it is God's way and wisdom.

Wisdom and Living Life

So, if we choose to trust in Christ, how can we live the life of wisdom God would have for us? Remember the definition of wisdom: applying God's truth to life in the power of the Holy Spirit. If we are going to embrace this definition of wisdom there are three things we need to do.

First, we need to know God's truth. God has graciously revealed his truth for us in his word. I love Deuteronomy 29:29 because of its practical advice for all who want to live a godly life of wisdom:

> The secret things belong to the Lord our God, but the things revealed belong to us and to our children forever, that we may follow all the words of this law. (NIV)

The things God has revealed are found in his Word. They are given to us so we can follow them in our day-to-day living. If we read God's Word, we will discover it has truth for all areas of life. God tells us the truth about ourselves, our family life, our financial life, our social life and our spiritual life. If we read the Bible and grow in our knowledge of this revealed truth we have taken the first step in a life of wisdom. But it is only the first step.

The second step is to apply the truth we know to the circumstances of life. Truth known is only valuable to us if it becomes truth lived. I have discovered in my life, and I think it is true for everyone, we know better than we do. We know the right thing to do in any given situation and often we do the right thing, but not always. I think most people listen to their conscience and therefore want to do the right thing. But unfortunately, we often fail in our attempt to do what we know is right. Why is that? Even the great Apostle Paul struggled with this reality. He knew what was right. He wanted to do what was right, but he often failed. He relates his struggle for us in Romans 7. Read Romans 7:21-25:

> [21]So I find it to be a law that when I want to do right, evil lies close at hand. [22]For I delight in the law of God, in my inner being, [23]but I see in my members another law waging war against the law of my mind and making me captive to the law of sin that dwells in my members. [24]Wretched man that I am! Who will deliver me from this body of death? [25]Thanks be to God through Jesus Christ our Lord! So then, I myself serve the law of God with my mind, but with my flesh I serve the law of sin. (ESV)

This second step in a life of wisdom is the application of God's truth to life, but it is a challenging step. We want to do what is right but we fail far more often than we like. Is there a solution to this challenge? Yes, Paul gives it to us in Romans 8.

The third step in living a life of wisdom is to apply God's truth to life in the power of the Holy Spirit. If we try to apply God's truth to life apart from the Holy Spirit, all we have is religion. When I was growing up, I found that religion didn't work when it came to empowering me to godly living. Religion prodded me to do the right thing. It made me feel guilty when I failed but it never empowered me from within to do the right thing. Paul seems to have discovered the same reality which he relates in Romans 7. Fortunately, God has the solution to this tragic situation. He has given us his Holy Spirit who enables us to apply God's truth to life if we will let Him. Paul relates this victory for us in Romans 8. I know this is a long passage but listen to Romans 8:5-13:

> [5] For those who live according to the flesh set their minds on the things of the flesh, but those who live according to the Spirit set their minds on the things of the Spirit. [6] For to set the mind on the flesh is death, but to set the mind on the Spirit is life and peace. [7] For the mind that is set on the flesh is hostile to God, for it does not submit to God's law; indeed, it cannot. [8] Those who are in the flesh cannot please God.
>
> [9] You, however, are not in the flesh but in the Spirit, if in fact the Spirit of God dwells in you. Anyone who does not have the Spirit of Christ does not belong to him. [10] But if Christ is in you, although the body is dead because of sin, the Spirit is life because of righteousness. [11] If the Spirit of him who raised Jesus from the dead dwells in you, he who raised Christ Jesus from the dead will also give life to your mortal bodies through his Spirit who dwells in you.
>
> [12] So then, brothers, we are debtors, not to the flesh, to live according to the flesh. [13] For if you live according to the flesh you

will die, but if by the Spirit you put to death the deeds of the body, you will live. (ESV)

Look at the last little paragraph above. As followers of Jesus Christ, recipients of God's Spirit, we are in debt not to the flesh but to the Spirit. In fact, we can now put to death the desires and deeds of the flesh and live a holy life in the power of the Spirit. Ask God to fill you with His Holy Spirit and see what happens.

Keep in mind this good advice from John Bunyan: Prayer will make a man cease from sin, or sin will entice a man to cease from prayer.

The human experience is a wonderful thing to behold. As participants in this experience, I would hope our desire is to enhance this life in the best ways we can. This brief book proposes the best way to enhance life is through a life-changing, personal faith in Jesus Christ. I realize this idea may seem simplistic, even foolish to many. That is not an unusual response to the message of Jesus Christ. In fact, this has been the case since the Gospel of Jesus Christ was first preached. Listen to the challenge the Apostle Paul faced as he proclaimed the good news concerning Jesus Christ in his day:

> [18]For the message of the cross is foolishness to those who are perishing, but it is God's power to us who are being saved. [19]For it is written:
> I will destroy the wisdom of the wise, and I will set aside the understanding of the experts.
> [20]Where is the philosopher? Where is the scholar? Where is the debater of this age? Hasn't God made the world's wisdom foolish? [21]For since, in God's wisdom, the world did not know God through wisdom, God was pleased to save those who believe through the foolishness of the message preached. [22]For the Jews ask for signs and the Greeks seek wisdom, [23]but we preach Christ

crucified, a stumbling block to the Jews and foolishness to the Gentiles. [24]Yet to those who are called, both Jews and Greeks, Christ is God's power and God's wisdom, [25]because God's foolishness is wiser than human wisdom, and God's weakness is stronger than human strength. (1 Corinthians 1:18-25 CSB)

A life of faith in Christ can and should lead to a life of true spiritual wisdom and spiritual power. Wisdom is something that the Bible tells us is for everyone. Listen to what the apostle James says:

"If any of you lacks wisdom, you should ask God, who gives generously to all without finding fault, and it will be given to you." (James 1:5 NIV)

Here's what Solomon says to us in Proverbs 3:13-14:

[13]Blessed are those who find wisdom, those who gain understanding, [14]for she is more profitable than silver, and yields better returns than gold. (NIV)

Our world needs true wisdom. I hope that you will be among those who find God's wisdom in your life and that this chapter has been helpful to that end.

Prophecy

Prophecy has always interested me, even when I was a child. Maybe that's because Jeane Dixon was popular in the 60's, who claimed to be a prophet of God. But she was a false prophet, since she was wrong more often than she was right. The press tended to report what she got right and skipped the rest. Still, on her deathbed at age 93, she did correctly say: "I knew this would happen."

Besides Dixon, who isn't going to take a second look at what Nostradamus has to say about any given year? However even he, with a name that's survived since the 1500's, wasn't more than 70% correct. Not so bad if you compare that to, let's say, a 70% chance of rain. I'd definitely bring an umbrella! But his prophecies are often so vague you really must struggle to match their supposed fulfillment.

Especially when you compare Dixon and Nostradamus with actual Biblical prophecy standards: **True prophets of God must be 100% correct.**

Why bother to talk about prophecy?

There are roughly 2500 prophecies in the Bible, with about 500 yet to be fulfilled (although some sources have slightly different counts, these numbers are taken from reasons.org). In fact, 27% of the Bible contains prophecy (this according to the book *Jesus on Trial* by David Limbaugh). It seems obvious to me that if a quarter of the Bible talks about one specific element, we ought to be hearing of it from the pulpit, investigating it ourselves, and/or talking about it.

Maybe God used prophecy of the past as a way for us to trust Him. Maybe those yet-to-be fulfilled prophecies are to help us prepare for what's ahead. Or maybe, as Jesus Himself said: "I have told you now before it happens so that when it does happen **you may believe**." (John 14:29 CSB)

Admittedly, many Bible prophecies employ symbols—which usually evoke more emotion than simple, straight forward words would (God is, among many other talents, a fantastic writer!). Unlike simple words which can change through the generations, symbolic language makes prophecy timeless. They're something that can be imagined throughout the ages. With a little digging to understand what symbols stand for in the context they were written, the mysteries give way to awe.

Historical Prophecy

In his book *Jesus on Trial*, lawyer and political commentator David Limbaugh devoted an entire chapter to fulfilled prophecy. I highly recommend having a look, because he analyzes a number of Old Testament prophecies about history, Christ's life and ministry, His death, His very nature, i.e. One who pre-existed His birth, names He would be called, His special anointing, His zeal for God's Temple.

Here are just a few of the prophecies, written well before their fulfillment, that I've paraphrased from Limbaugh's book:

- **Sojourners and Slaves**, prophecy of the hundreds of years of Jewish slavery in Egypt, as well as their deliverance. (Genesis 15:13-16)

- **The fall of Israel and punishment of Assyria**, here Limbaugh details Israel first as a united kingdom and then divided into two parts, northern (Israel) and southern (Judah). Predictions about the destruction of the northern kingdom came first, by the Assyrians, and that the southern kingdom would be conquered by the Babylonians, along with their exile to Babylon. (Isaiah 9:8-10:4, among others)
- **Cyrus and the end of the Babylonian exile**, "Cyrus" would allow the rebuilding of Solomon's Temple which the Babylonians had destroyed. (Isaiah 44:24-28) At the time of Isaiah's prophecy, the people of Israel weren't even in captivity, and Cyrus wouldn't be born for another 100 years. Unbelievable? Perhaps a much later addition to the Book of Isaiah? The Dead Sea Scrolls provided a complete copy of Isaiah, dating far older (minimum 125 BC) than any copy of Scripture we had, disproving some of the later dates that skeptics tried to assign. Although the dates of the scrolls are still after Daniel lived, they are based on *already established* texts and traditions. The Dead Sea Scrolls proved how amazingly unchanged our current Scripture is, because "... it is the true word of God, handed down without essential loss from generation to generation throughout the centuries." (Sir Frederic Kenyon, 1863-1952, author of *Our Bible and the Ancient Manuscripts*.)
- **Bethlehem** to be the Messiah's birth place. (Micah 5:2)
- **The rebuilding of Jerusalem** is prophesied, including measurements, along with the **re-gathering of Israel** to the land (Israel became a nation again in 1948, was then attacked and became stunningly victorious in subsequent wars of 1967 and 1973). The Jewish people were scattered twice before that, as prophesied—once for the 70 years after being conquered by Babylon, then again in 70 AD when Rome conquered them. They

were scattered until 1948. (Jeremiah 25:11 and Deuteronomy 28:64-68) Persecution was also predicted for these scattered Jews, which culminated in World War II. (See the "trampling down by Gentiles" in Luke 21:24) After the Romans destroyed Jerusalem and along with it the second temple, it would be nearly 2000 years before they were re-gathered and able to rebuild modern-day Jerusalem as outlined in the book of Jeremiah. (Ezekiel 37:21-28 and Isaiah 11:11-12) How many generations pass in 2000 years? Josh McDowell says history shows a national people group would disappear after about five generations (being conquered and then through assimilation). God's chosen people kept their identity, traditions, beliefs, etc., and survived what other nations couldn't except for the hand of God.

- **The demise of Edom,** formerly a lush and fertile land that would be obliterated as described in Obadiah, Jeremiah and Ezekiel. To this day, this portion of Jordan is bleak and desolate. (Obadiah and Jeremiah 49:15-20, Ezekiel 25:12-14)
- **The destruction of Tyre and Nineveh.** (Ezekiel 26:3-4 for Tyre and several spots for Nineveh's destruction: Nahum 1-3, Zephaniah 2:13-15, Zechariah 10:11, Isaiah 10:12-19, 14:24-25, 30:31-33, 31:8-9) Nineveh was in ancient Assyria, and archeology verified the ruins of this city in 1845.
- **Josiah** (a future king of Israel named specifically) and the **bones of the pagan priests** that would be sacrificed on King Jeroboam's altar (300 years prior to fulfillment). 1 Kings 13:1-3, fulfilled 2 Kings 23:15-17)

Prophecies foretold about Christ's first coming
Here's a brief list of some of my favorites. There are many others

which anyone can easily access online (just search prophecy in the Bible, Old Testament prophecies Jesus fulfilled, etc.)

- Jesus came through the line of David. Biblical genealogy is always paternal, so this is Joseph's line as the chosen earthly father to the Messiah. / **Foretold:** 2 Samuel 7:12-13, Jeremiah 33:14-15, Ezekiel 34:23-24, Ezekiel 37:24-25 / **Fulfilled:** Matthew 1:1-16
- Jesus would be meek and lowly. / **Foretold:** Isaiah 42:1-4 / **Fulfilled:** Matthew 12:15-21
- Jesus would arrive in Jerusalem on a donkey and greeted as King to "praises of Hosanna." **Foretold:** Zechariah 9:9 / **Fulfilled:** Matthew 21:6-10, John 12:12-13
- He'd be hated without cause. **Foretold:** Psalm 35:19, Psalm 69:4 / **Fulfilled:** John 15:24-25
- Betrayed for 30 pieces of silver/money cast in the House of the Lord. **Foretold:** Zechariah 11:12-13 / **Fulfilled:** Matthew 26:14-15, Matthew 27:3-5
- He'd be silent before accusers. **Foretold:** Isaiah 53:7 / **Fulfilled:** Matthew 27:12-14
- He would hang cursed on a tree. **Foretold:** Deuteronomy 21:23, / **Fulfilled:** Acts 13:29-33
- His body would be pierced. **Foretold:** Psalm 22:14&16, Zechariah 12:10 / **Fulfilled:** John 19:34-37
- But not a bone would be broken. **Foretold:** Exodus 12:46, Numbers 9:12, Psalm 34:20 / **Fulfilled:** John 19:31-36
- He'd be given vinegar for His thirst. **Foretold:** Psalm 69:21 / **Fulfilled:** Matthew 27:34
- They would divide and cast lots for His clothing. **Foretold:** Psalm 22:18 / **Fulfilled:** John 19:23-24
- Messiah would be abandoned by those closest to Him. **Foretold:** Psalm 41:9 / **Fulfilled:** John 13:18
- Buried in a rich man's grave. **Foretold:** Isaiah 53:9 / **Fulfilled:** Matthew 27:57-60

These are just a sampling of the prophecies foretold about Jesus, His life and sacrificial death. For a more detailed list you can download a table from: <u>351 Old Testament Prophecies Fulfilled in Jesus Christ</u>.

The point here is that there are an amazing number of fulfilled prophecies regarding Christ. The prophecies were given to various people in various places and at various times (centuries apart, centuries before Christ's birth), yet they intertwine and all came true.

Many prophecies about the Messiah are found in Isaiah (many more than I've listed), and verified by the Dead Sea Scrolls as having been written well before Jesus was born. These prophecies were not "added later" or manipulated by devious people trying to prove something; they are authentic, 100% correct, prophecies about Jesus' first coming—and awe inspiring!

A note about why the Jewish people don't accept Jesus as the Messiah: they were expecting a political figure who would overturn the Romans, the government in authority over Jews at the time. On Palm Sunday the disciples thought they were on target when Jesus came into Jerusalem to so many people crying out Hosanna! They thought He'd start His reign on earth. Instead, He was crucified, which is why the disciples feared they'd gotten it wrong and went into hiding immediately after His arrest.

However, the conquering Jesus describes Christ's *second* coming, when He does overthrow the world government being run by antichrist. (More about that later.)

As an intro to my favorite prophecies from the Book of Daniel, I'll start with this one: Daniel predicted the Messiah's public ministry would be 483 years after the decree to restore Jerusalem and rebuild the temple that had been destroyed by Nebuchadnezzar. The decree was issued by Artexerxes in 458 BC, and 483 years later people welcomed Jesus into Jerusalem on Palm Sunday.

Additional Prophecy already fulfilled

Daniel's interpretation of King Nebuchadnezzar's dream, found in Daniel Chapter 2, is among the most fascinating. (Nebuchadnezzar was the Babylonian king who conquered Judah and took many Jews to Babylonia as slaves.)

First let me pause to say a bit about prophecy, and specifically about the Book of Daniel itself. Generally speaking, skeptics have a hard time accepting the supernatural element of the Bible and in particular Jesus, whom both the Old and New Testaments talk about. After all, if the Bible just told of a good teacher who went around preaching God's love but never mentioned anything supernatural (miracles, resurrection, being God) then they would be happy to extol the records about an admirable historical figure.

It's only the supernatural parts that raise objections. I understand that. But I still believe archeology has proven Scripture should be trusted, including the supernatural parts, because of the consistency and reliability of the witnesses proclaiming not just the history but also the supernatural parts. If you believe there is a spiritual realm, as I do, then these well-documented accounts can also be true.

Now about Daniel specifically. For around 800 years, this book was accepted as sacred. Then, in the 3rd century AD an atheist philosopher named Porphyry, in his appropriately named book *"Against the Christian,"* proclaimed that Daniel must be a fraud, because no one could be as accurate as he was about forthcoming events. Because of his skepticism, Porphyry said the book was likely written in the second century BC. This would have been well after most of the prophecies were fulfilled.

Also, he said, Daniel was written in Hebrew (Daniel's native language) and Aramaic (the language of the Babylonians which he would have had to learn after his exile to Babylon), as well as Greek. Greek, said Porphyry, wasn't spoken in this region. Trouble is, he doesn't bother to mention that the three Greek words he referred to were musical instruments commonly sold back in the actual area and era Daniel himself claimed to have lived. Daniel used contemporaneous words in use in the era and region for goods that could have been bought or brought from areas where these instruments originated.

Speaking of words in use at the time, if you've lived long enough you know words and their meanings can change even in one generation. "Sick" used to mean you don't feel well. Now it means "cool!" "Bad" used to mean... well, bad. Now, it means "even better than good" to some people a whole lot younger than me. (That's an observation from J. Warner Wallace.) Besides these examples, when I was researching legal terms associated with "feebleminded" in use during the 1800s for my book *On Sparrow Hill*, I found it interesting that words like "imbecile" and "lunatic" began as legal terms. In a hundred years or so they evolved into the derogatory words we know today, just as "bad" seems to be evolving into something "good."

This has always been the case with language, including the language Daniel used. Words commonly used in the 6th century BC (when this is dated) were no longer used the same way in the 2nd century BC in the Babylonian region, yet the language and dialect used in Daniel represents the 6th century BC and not the language of four hundred years later in the 2nd century BC Babylonia.

Porphyry also claimed Daniel got some history wrong, saying Belshazzar wasn't a king, as Daniel called him. Technically, Belshazzar was a co-regent because his father, King Nabonidus, spent nearly a decade either on the battlefield or in other faraway places. This left Belshazzar at home to rule. Legal deeds from this time sometimes included an oath by gods and king, and history reveals documents referring to both Nabonidus and Belshazzar as king.

Belshazzar was also called the son of Nebuchadnezzar, not allowing for the word "father" and "grandfather" to be used in more general terms (Jesus was a son of David, for example). Those in power were Nabonidus, his son Belshazzar, and then Daniel as "the third" in power just as Daniel's text explains.

Proverbs, Ecclesiastes and Ezekiel were all challenged at one point or another, but Daniel wasn't challenged until Porphyry came along. If the Ancient Synagogues and the Sanhedrin, a group known for study, pursuit of truth, especially reverent and conservative, accepted the Book of Daniel as Scripture, why should we, so many years later, doubt it?

Few people took Porphyry to heart until more modern times as general skepticism in supernatural elements spread.

Besides all that, Ezekiel mentions Daniel three times, as a righteous man. Ezekiel wasn't challenged as Scripture by Jewish scholars. Why would someone try to make Daniel into a fraud?

More importantly, why would Jesus Himself either perpetrate the lie or fall for it, when He quoted Daniel? (Matthew 24:15)

Then there is the first century historian Josephus, who referred to Daniel having been written in the 6th century BCE. Was secular Josephus spreading a lie as well, when one of his stated goals was to record knowledge of what actually happened in history, without deference to any faith?

So here's the scoop about one of my favorite prophecies from Daniel:

King Nebuchadnezzar has a bad night's sleep, so he calls in his worldly astrologers to demand they interpret his troubling dream—something even *he* can't properly recall. The astrologers ask for some details, but he won't, or can't, give them any. He accuses them of being quacks if they can't figure out this dream as well as its interpretation. What's he paying them for, anyway, if not for divination? They say (respectfully, I'm sure!) that not a man on this earth could do what the King demanded. So the King did what evil Kings did in those days and orders them all to be killed.

But Daniel hears about it and asks God to help so he can save these poor souls, his own among them since Daniel was also an adviser and subject to the king's punishment. He asks King Nebbie for a little time, which is granted. That night Daniel also has a dream—mirroring Nebuchadnezzar's. Daniel wakes knowing he's able to do what the others failed to do. He hurries over to the King, begging for no one to be killed over this. He has the answer the King was looking for.

Basically Nebuchadnezzar's dream was of a statue of a man made from five different materials. As you'll see below, a second reference to this dream interpretation is found in Daniel Chapter 7. In that chapter, Daniel's dream gives a little more symbolic detail, and the five empires represented by different materials in Chapter 2 are represented by animals in Chapter 7.

Keep in mind that Daniel was taken as a slave to Babylon in **605 BC**, and although he served under the then-King Nebuchadnezzar, Daniel lived there until he was an old man, witnessing the beginning of the *next* Empire in 538/9 BC. As you'll see, I guess he wasn't surprised when Cyrus came with the Medes and Persians to crush the Babylonians, Egyptians and Libyans! No one could have foreseen so many more empires, except through a vision from God.

Following is the interpretation of Nebuchadnezzar's dream of the statue of a man, as prophetically revealed to Daniel:

The Babylonian Empire: 606 - 561 BC

The Head in Chapter 2 of Gold is symbolized as a Lion in Chapter 7, because for a little while Nebuchadnezzar went crazy and lived like a beast before coming back to his senses. (Predicted in Daniel 4:16, fulfilled Daniel 4:33.) Historically, this Empire is linked to carvings of Lions, which archeology has confirmed.

The Medes and Persians, 538 BC

The Arms and Chest of the statue are silver, represented in Chapter 7 as a bear with three ribs in its mouth, each rib representing one of the three empires that were conquered: Babylon, Egypt, and Libya. A "leaning" bear because the power leans toward the Persians; eventually history refers to this era as the **Persian Empire.**

Grecian Empire, Alexander the Great, 330 BC

The thighs of the statue in Chapter 2 are Brass, depicted as a Leopard in Chapter 7, because the leopard was the fastest animal known. The entire Persian Empire would fall quickly (in just 3 years). This leopard has four heads because Alexander died shortly thereafter and his power was split between four generals from: Greece, Asia Minor, Persia, and Egypt.

Roman Empire, 146 BC, split into Eastern and Western Empires

The two legs of the Roman Empire are depicted as Iron in Chapter 2 and as "A frightening and dreadful beast" because it was fierce, strong and long-lasting.

The Future Empire during End Times

The Feet are made of Clay and Iron which don't mix and so are weak. There is no animal symbolism, perhaps because this last period of human history comes out of the Western culture founded by the Roman Empire and therefore would still be represented by the dreadful beast. I believe the divisiveness throughout the world today could represent this situation of clay and iron not mixing. The ten toes represent 10 horns from Revelation 13 as the strongest nations during that time, yet to come.

A Stone.

The final material mentioned in Daniel 2 is a stone which is cast at the statue, crushing it. This stone will not be cut by human hand, and represents Jesus as He ends this last human empire. He'll replace it with His Kingdom for the Millennium Age.

History has proven Daniel's prophecy to be 100% correct, with only the toes yet to be fulfilled.

I also love that the Bible authenticates itself. Another Biblical prophet, Isaiah, said the conqueror with the Medes and Persians would be named Cyrus, who would decide to let the Jews who were exiled under the Babylonians go free without any payment/ransom. (Isaiah 44:28, 45:1 and 45:13) This was 150 years before Cyrus was born, 180 years before Cyrus did any of this, and 80 years before the Jews were even taken into exile.

Do you know what the chances are that Isaiah could have predicted this without God's help? According to Hugh Ross of

Reasons to Believe (reasons.org) the probability of fulfillment for this is 1 in 10 to the 15th power—that's one chance in 10 with 15 zeroes after it!

It's this kind of confirmation that gives authority and authenticity to the Bible, and strengthens my faith.

But wait! I can see certain people shaking their head again, even if I add that historical figures like Plato and Pliny the Elder helped authenticate the age and consistency of Scripture, not to mention the hundreds of copies that have been found with very few content variants. History itself verifies Scripture as accurate, and written when it claims to have been written—prior to the fulfillment of prophecies.

There's more documentation supporting the New Testament than any other ancient manuscript, and in many senses (because there are so many Old Testament references) the New Testament alone is verification of the Old Testament.

Still, I can see it would be hard to accept the fantastic idea that the Bible predicts the end of the world—even if some people do concede that someday, somehow, there probably will be an end. After all, if the Universe had a beginning, it stands to reason there will be an end. Maybe it'll end naturally because we're expanding and can't live too far from the sun, or the Sun will burn so hot it'll no longer sustain life—a climate change crisis. Or perhaps it will end prematurely via a nuclear disaster, or an asteroid. We'll get into more detail later, but let me just say that climate change, nuclear disasters and asteroids will likely play a part in ending this current age and ushering in the next.

A brief history of Israel

One of the most amazing, and fulfilled prophecies is that Israel exists as a country, after 2000 years. This, probably more than any other prophecy, shows that God keeps His promises. Scripture says He would regather His people before end times. (Deuteronomy

30:1-5, Isaiah 41:8-9, Ezekiel 20:33-38, Ezekiel 22:17-22, Jeremiah 30:10, among others.)

The idea of Israel as a country started when God told Abram (Abraham) to leave his family and homeland to go to the Promised Land (then called the land of the Canaanites). God promised Abraham's descendants, the Hebrews, they would possess this land forever. (Genesis 15:18) It all started out so . . . well, promisingly! In the beginning, Abraham believed God's promise and settled in Canaan, but he had no children. In an attempt to help God complete His promise of children, Abraham and Hagar had Ishmael whose lineage led to the Arabs, then Muhammed and ultimately Islam. Finally, in God's timing, and in their old age, Abraham and Sarah had Isaac, whose lineage led to the Jewish nation (Israel) and eventually to Jesus. Israel has a long and tumultuous history, and despite wars, captivity, slavery and being scattered twice, there have always been at least some Jews living in the land now called Israel.

Although Abraham moved to Israel around 2000 BC, the glory days were during King David's reign beginning in 1000 BC. Following David was his son, King Solomon who built the first temple (completed in 957 BC). The temple in Jerusalem was built on Mount Moriah, the very spot where God tells Abraham to bring Isaac for the near-sacrifice. After King Solomon's rule the country of Israel split into two parts: the Northern part was called Israel/Samaria and the southern part called Judea.

By 722 BC the Assyrians conquered Israel's northern kingdom and scattered the people (Samaritans) from that part of Israel. Then, the Babylonian Empire under King Nebuchadnezzar conquered the southern part of Israel (Judea) and put many of its people (the Jews) into exile in Babylon. In 586 BC, the Babylonian Empire destroyed the original Jewish temple that King Solomon built.

Seven decades later, when Cyrus conquered the Babylonians (heralding the Medes and Persians Empire) many Jews returned to Israel. In 516 BC the Jews built the second temple using the foundation of the first. This second temple was relatively modest compared to the grandeur of Solomon's. After several centuries of various conquerors, the Roman Empire conquered Israel in 63 BC. The Roman ally, King Herod was put in charge in 37 BC and started expanding the second temple in 19 BC. Jesus was soon born and ministered to the Jews, ultimately predicting this second temple would be destroyed. The Jews revolted against the Romans in 66 AD and the Romans reconquered Judea. They destroyed the second temple in 70 AD and the Jews were driven out and scattered once again.

In 135 AD, when the Jews fought again with the Romans, Roman Emperor Hadrian wasn't satisfied with just quelling this rebellion. He wanted to erase all memory of the Jews, so he banished them from Judea. He then renamed the area Palestine, a derivative of "Philistine" as an insult to the Jews. Philistine was a common (derogatory) name for "uncivilized" enemies of Israel. From this point on, everyone living in Israel would be called Palestinian, including Jews, Christians and Arabs, even though an official nation of Palestine was never established.

Between the Romans and modern-day Israel, there were many struggles for God's holy land. The Byzantines, Arabs, Catholic Crusades, Muslim Mamluks, Muslim Ottomans and British, all claimed control at one point or another during the next 1900 years, oppressing any remaining Jews. Control of Israel began and ended the same way other lands have been taken over through history: by military conquest, the last such conquest being Britain's in 1917. This land, however, originally belonged to the Jews and they lived there for many centuries prior to the Romans up through to the British, as archeology proves. As long ago as the 13th century BC, the Egyptian Merneptah Stele refers to "Israel" as its own nation, and after that (9th Century BC) the Tel Dan Stele refers to King David and corroborates rulers in 2 Kings which refer to the Land of Israel.

Although the majority of Jews were scattered to all "four corners of the world," they continued to maintain the Jewish culture and tradition. This allowed natural cohesion for those who ultimately returned.

In the late 1880s, when Israel/Palestine was still part of the Ottoman Empire, the Jewish Zionist movement started, for Jews to return to their homeland. In large part this was a reaction to persecution and pogroms (officially sanctioned massacres), inspiring Jews from all over the world to want to reestablish Israel as their official home. Older Jews began returning to spend their last years in Jerusalem and Jewish families moved back to work the land. They even revived the Hebrew language.

After the First World War when Britain conquered the Ottomans, British authorities favored the re-establishment of a Jewish nation. So, many more Jews began returning, although for a time Britain put a limit on that to appease the large Muslim population. But the Zionist movement wanted to show that Arabs and Jews could live side-by-side. This proved more difficult than expected. There were riots and tensions between the Muslim population and newly returning Jews, especially as more Muslims started moving to Israel once it began to flourish, leaving its "wasteland" days forever behind.

On May 14, 1948, Britain (peacefully) handed over control to the Jews and they are once again in charge of the land God gave them. Through centuries of persecution and pogroms, God nonetheless miraculously preserved His chosen people, which is why I included this very abbreviated history. This is one of the most important fulfilled prophecies because Scripture explicitly states the Jews would be "gathered" back in Israel at the time of Jesus' return.

Future Prophecy

Mostly just for fun, I'm going to dive into the topic of end times prophecy. (Insert eyeroll here for those readers who are doing so only to be polite or because someone guilted them into spending time in this book. Ah-hem.)

What does this have to do with defending my faith, you might ask? Actually, not much. I do, however, find it fascinating because the nature of so many prophecies yet to be fulfilled couldn't have been figured out even 100 years ago, let alone 2,000 or more. I find it faith-building to see just how far-sighted the Bible has proven to be.

Besides, if so many Biblical prophecies have already been fulfilled, why doubt the ones that are still on the horizon? Jesus said He's coming back (Luke 21:27-28 among many other verses). Why doubt it? He said there will be an end to the world as we know it (Mark 13:7, Luke 21:9 and Matthew 24:6 & 14). Why doubt it?

The Bible tells us in 2nd Peter 3:10 that God will dissolve this earth by fire. He did, after all, promise not to destroy mankind by flood again, but never said He wouldn't use fire. Not to worry! He's preparing a new heaven and new earth for those of us who want to spend eternity with Him. Based on the wonders of this world I'm sure an updated version will be spectacular!

Jesus said He's coming as a "thief in the night" and even though we can't know the exact date or year, those who will be most surprised when He returns are the ones not looking for the signs.

Let me say something else before anyone tosses this little book aside as the rantings of a lunatic. Although I do believe current events seem to be preparing the world for some really dramatic end time prophecies, I know with just as much certainty that I *don't* know when all these prophecies will take place. I might be around for end time events, or end time events might begin long after I'm gone. Who knows, but God Himself?

I'm also proposing that today's technologies provide many avenues to fulfill end time prophecy. However, if you've lived longer than ten minutes you know technology marches on. Even though we already have simple means for certain things to happen does not mean there won't be even simpler means in the future. Just having the technology available as never before is not necessarily an end times indicator. It does mean we're able to imagine some end time prophecies that would have been unimaginable when God first revealed them.

One other note before continuing. Why would God want to bring an end to human history as we know it? To me, the answer is because He gave us free will. He didn't create robots, made to love Him without a choice. But that ability to choose led us to need a Savior, since God's perfection prevents Him from fellowshipping with those prone to sin, like us. Ultimately, His goal is to be rid of evil and suffering. That's why this world will come to an end, so we can enjoy an eternity of fellowship with God and everyone else who wants to be with Him.

Now back to the subject at hand. The Bible compares signs of end times to birth pangs. Unless you're like my friend Donna who delivered her daughter in record time, birth pangs usually start out relatively mild. They gradually increase in intensity and eventually come closer together until the birth. For some women, like me, the big event starts with "practice pangs" called Braxton-Hicks. They don't do much except let the mom-to-be know the uterus is getting ready for the real thing. Personally, I think we might be in the Braxton-Hicks phase of human history. The following list contains prophecies indicating the end isn't upon us but might be "drawing near."

- As mentioned previously, Israel had to be an official homeland again before Jesus returns. Lots of passages reflect the prophetic "regathering" of Jews. (Besides those mentioned, see also Isaiah 11:11-12 and Amos 9:14-15.) This prophecy for the Jews was fulfilled in 1948.
- Israel, just prior to what's called the 7 year Tribulation period that will be the final seven years of history as we know it, must be prosperous, and will bloom. (Isaiah 27:6 and 35:1-2, Ezekiel 36:30-36, 38:12-13) Before Israel became a nation in 1948, Mark Twain traveled the area and called Palestine "a wasteland" and "without a tree to be found." But Israel today is certainly prosperous, and even great for farming. It's ranked among the top economies in the world. By the way, since 1949 Israel has planted at least 250,000 trees, and

rainfall levels have remained the same despite climate change (based on a study conducted between 1952 and 2006). Trees fight climate change! (Prophecy about the trees: Isaiah 41:19-20)
- Israel will experience an unprecedented peace just prior to the Tribulation. As I write this chapter, the Palestinian terrorist group, Hamas, which controls the Gaza Strip in Israel, has attacked and killed many hundreds of Jews and taken scores of civilians and soldiers hostage. There is currently no peace in Israel, and anti-Israel sentiments are increasing worldwide. Prior to this, however, the Abraham Accords were a good example of an "unprecedented peace." Is this Hamas war just another in the long string of attacks Israel has had to endure, or will this current break from previous peace lead to what's called the Gog-Magog war of Ezekiel 38 & 39, signaling end times? No one can tell where this war will lead or how long it will last, but as long as surrounding countries, including Russia who is allied with Iran, don't get involved, the answer is no, this is not the Gog-Magog war. That said, even if this Hamas war is short lived (God willing!) the foundation might be set for an expanded attack against Israel, especially when Israel's defense proves successful and peace is restored.
- Prior to 1967 there were no Messianic Congregations; today there are more than 350, one hundred of them in Israel. The Gentile Age ended once Jews regained control of Jerusalem (after the 6-Day War in 1967). Since then, God has been softening the hearts of many Jews. (Romans 11:25 and Luke 21:24)
- Organizations like the World Economic Forum, World Trade Organization, World Health Organization, World Climate Foundation, the United Nations/NATO, European Union, the World Bank, the World

Federation (an Islamic faith-based organization aiming to gather all faiths for humanitarian work) and PGI (Partnership for Global Infrastructure and Investment, similar to China's Belt and Road Initiative to make globalization practical) and others are precursors to a one-world government that will be necessary for end times. (Revelation 13:7-8) Nations have often embraced strong leaders, and right now everyone seems to be looking for leadership that can coordinate organizations like these as a foundation for a global government. It's the perfect opportunity for an antichrist to rise.

- During the Tribulation period, all commerce will be tightly controlled. No one will be able to buy or sell anything unless they have the "mark of the beast," which means money will no longer be available in the anonymous bills we carry in our pockets. Crypto, anyone? (Revelation 13:17)
- Technology like biometric surveillance (chips) inserted into the forehead or hand will make it possible to receive this "mark of the beast" as described in Revelation 13. Without it, people won't be able to buy or sell during end times. I've recently heard about DARPA (part of our Department of Defense: Defense Advanced Research Projects Agency) which as long as ten years ago investigated chips to be inserted just under the skin either invisibly or "designer"—i.e. a tattoo, for personal identification. They were also looking into ingestible pills, a technology the size of a couple grains of sand, that can be activated by stomach acids to "map our body signature." We'd be a walking wallet. It's meant to be a security measure to prevent identity theft or bank fraud or for convenience to instantly access our personal computers, even to stop human trafficking. All good possibilities. But it's incredible that the Bible predicted an individual identification method as a numbers-based

system that will be used to control who can participate in any kind of commerce. Numbers run all of our computers. Antichrist will likely attach his number (666) to each person (social security or license or some new ID number) in order to identify and track his followers. Accepting this mark will be a new, intentional act of allegiance to antichrist, and those who refuse will be social outcasts in a very dire way.
- If Covid-19 taught world governments anything, it was how to instill fear into the general population, taking away basic freedoms and gaining greater control over people.
- Birth pangs before the "days of sorrow" (Tribulation) describe wars and rumors of wars. (Mark 13:7-8) There were 29 nations at war when I started this book in the spring of 2023, though now we only hear about Ukraine, and more recently the Hamas war in Israel.
- There will be an increase in travel and knowledge. (Daniel 12:4) Mankind is traveling with unprecedented ease and in greater number than ever before in human history. And Internet knowledge certainly isn't wisdom, but it has definitely broadened our grasp of information in a way never before seen.
- There will be a rise in deception and confusion. (Matthew 24:24, 1 Timothy 4:1, 2 Timothy 3:13 and 4:3-4) The Internet is a quick way to spread lies and confusion, and the world media has probably never been trusted less than it is today. Nearly everyone asks: what's true? What's part of an agenda? What only *appears* authentic? The rise of Artificial Intelligence has provided the opportunity to take deception farther than it has ever been before—and may be of special use to the antichrist.
- Although there will be dramatic earthquakes, flooding, massive hail and terrible wonders in the sky

during the actual Tribulation period, earthquakes have been on the rise in recent years. Are these birth pangs warning of greater tectonic shifts yet to come? (Matthew 24:7, Luke 21:11) Plus, Israel sits on the Syrian-African fault line, and it's said they experience a "significant" earthquake about every 100 years. The last big earthquake in Israel was 1927—almost 100 years ago.

- There will be a rise in antagonism toward Christianity. (2 Timothy 3:12) Even in America, a nation founded on Judeo-Christian values, Christianity is the one safe religion to attack. But around the world, the World Watch List from Open Doors (a Christian watch organization) and the Vatican both report growing levels of persecution and discrimination against Christians. Nigeria is currently the most dangerous place on earth for Christians.

- Although there will be a revival of faith like never before during the Tribulation, leading up to that point there will be a departure of faith first. (1 Timothy 4:1, 2 Timothy 3:1-5) This seems especially true right now, at least in Western culture. Although Christianity is still the largest faith group in the world, Islam has surpassed Christianity's growth. According to the Pew Research Center, by 2050 Muslims are expected to match the number of Christians worldwide. Churches in Europe and Canada are empty. Fewer people than ever identify as Christians here in the U.S. Our culture seems embarrassed by claims that our country's founders were Christians.

The above list isn't as long as it could be if I allowed more room, but these are the ones I found most intriguing. They seem either already fulfilled or could be fulfilled in the blink of an eye, based on the birth pangs we're instructed to look for. What other ancient book foresaw things which so closely match what the world has become?

You might also notice that Israel is mentioned often. That's because the last seven years of human history are Israel-centered. This is a sort of bookend to the history of God's chosen people: created to provide a Savior to the world, then in the end dealt with for rebellion while opening the eyes of many people (especially Jews but also Gentiles) before the final day.

I've used certain "end time" vocabulary words, and it's likely most people reading this have either heard of or know these words and meanings. Just so we're all on the same page, here are a few definitions:

The Rapture: (Revelation 3:10, Matthew 24:30-31, Luke 17:34-36, Daniel 12:1, 1 Corinthians 15:51-53, 1 Thessalonians 4:16-18, 1 Thessalonians 5:2, among others.) This is when Christians who are alive at the time will be "caught up" and taken to the clouds, immediately after the dead in Christ are resurrected from their graves. The souls of Christians who have already died are in heaven—to be absent from the body is to be with the Lord in heaven, 2 Corinthians 5:8. At the Rapture they will be resurrected, reuniting their souls with their earthly bodies. Every Christian will be involved in the Rapture, either from the grave or those still alive at the time. The Rapture is not the second coming of Jesus, since He doesn't actually return to earth for this event. Only Believers will see Him waiting for us up in the clouds. His actual second coming, at the pinnacle of the final war called Armageddon, will be seen by everyone—that's the second coming.

There are varying beliefs within the church regarding the Rapture. Some believe it will happen just before the Tribulation, bringing the Church Age to an end. This would spare Believers from all the trouble of the Tribulation. 1 Thessalonians 5:9 says: *For God has not destined us for wrath*, and that will certainly be a time of God's wrath. A few verses before that, from the same chapter: 1 Thessalonians 5:2-3 describe "peace and security" just before the Lord will come for us. Will there be peace and security at any time except *before* the Tribulation? Also, in Luke 17:26-27 Jesus compares end times to Noah's. Amid world-wide wickedness (perhaps similar to modern times?) those around Noah were enjoying banquets and parties and weddings right up to the beginning of the flood. Will anyone be enjoying life once the Tribulation begins, including the first three-and-a-half years so full of calamity, even if such calamity is more natural than supernatural? Noah was spared from the flood, why wouldn't we be spared from this? There are other verses that point to a "Pre-Trib" rapture, but this topic could fill books, so I'll leave it there.

Others believe the Rapture will take place *during* the Tribulation, before God's wrath is actually released. While those who hold a "Pre-Trib" Rapture believe this entire seven year period is God's wrath on a rebellious world, those who hold a "Pre-Wrath" Rapture believe the Tribulation begins with Satan's wrath, not God's. As alluded to above, the "beginning of sorrows," or the beginning of this tumultuous time, is more about natural disasters than supernatural judgments (see the Judgments, below). Believers will still be spared God's wrath, but they will experience at least the first half of the Tribulation period.

Still others believe the Rapture will occur afterward, at the same time Christ returns during Armageddon. That would require Believers to experience God's wrath which seems contradictory to Scripture.

This is one of those things, like the age of the Universe, that can be contentious among faithful Believers. Personally, I lean toward a Pre-Trib Rapture simply because even if the first few years are Satan's or even the antichrist's wrath, it's still wrath and the Bible says we're not destined for wrath. And as people suffer the terrible earthquake of the 6th Seal (which takes place relatively early in this 7 year period) they call it the wrath of the Lamb. And finally, because the Church is not mentioned again during the Tribulation, I believe the Church won't be here.

The timing of the Rapture, like the "old earth" versus "young earth" question, is not a core tenet of Christianity. It's my belief we'll all meet in heaven just after the Rapture, whenever it occurs, and be so filled with love for one another we won't care who was right or wrong. (Oh for the day when that love is here on earth!)

The Tribulation: a 7 year period of judgments on a rebellious world, with particular focus on Israel. It's a time of trouble as the world has never seen before (Daniel 12:1). The first three-and-a-half years will be relatively calm, even though there will be incredible natural disasters, war, and plagues that will result in many deaths. Compared to the second three-and-a-half years, it's not quite a piece of cake but is far less horrific. The second half will be so bad the days have to be cut short for the sake of those remaining people who become Believers.

Antichrist: A (human) man, chosen by Satan, who rises out of obscurity to eventually rule a one-world government. It's said, since Satan doesn't know when the last days will arrive, that he has chosen such a man during every generation in history just to be ready. Antiochus IV Epiphanes from the Book of Daniel is a precursor of the things Satan will do through the antichrist to gain power and turn people from the One True God.

- Antichrist is one part of the unholy trinity, mimicking the Father, Son, and Holy Spirit. This "trinity" will be Satan, Antichrist and False Prophet (who will protect and promote the antichrist).
- He will come out of one of the ten most prominent nations existing during the end times.
- He'll unseat three of the leaders from those ten nations, suggesting three of the ten nations are relatively weak.
- He'll sign a 7 year treaty with Israel, strengthening any existing peace. For this he'll be known as a "man of peace" as depicted in one of the 4 horsemen of the

apocalypse. This 7 year treaty might bring an end to all conflict in the Middle East, or even to settle another future, sudden attack on Israel foreseen as the Gog-Magog war which I mentioned earlier. It's important to know that antichrist will break this treaty halfway through the Tribulation (after three-and-a-half years) because this white horseman (antichrist) "went forth conquering and to conquer."

- He may receive a head wound at some point, (perhaps from an assassination attempt?) and believed to be dead but will be miraculously healed. (Mimicking the resurrection.)
- The false prophet will erect a statue of antichrist for people to worship. This happens at the half-way point in the Tribulation and is called the Abomination of Desolation. Perhaps this is where AI will come to its heyday because the statue will "talk," or exhibit some form of *artificial consciousness* as some in the tech world predict as an eventual goal for AI. According to Zechariah, antichrist will kill two-thirds of the Jews at this point, so when this abomination happens, the remaining believing Jews in Jerusalem should flee to sanctuary.
- As proof of the loyalty antichrist demands, everyone must receive the mark of the beast (administered by the false prophet). The mark is the number 666, perhaps a prefix to all personal IDs. This will require willing submission, acknowledging this man as a "god". (Think North Korea here, where the people revere their "beloved" leaders as god-like.) No one who receives this mark will be deceived about the pledge they're taking. A huge incentive to submit is that no one will be able to buy or sell without this mark, likely resulting in death by starvation for many people who believe in Christ during this period.

- He will be given authority to persecute Believers, not just Jews, including beheading them (a form of death which Isis, and more recently Hamas, has reminded us about).

The false prophet: As you've already guessed, he's the antichrist's sidekick, pointing people to the antichrist. He'll be meek and likable, but be the final, best example of what Christ said about false prophets in Matthew 7:15: *Beware of false prophets, which come to you in sheep's clothing, but inwardly they are ravenous wolves.* (KJV) The false prophet will perform miracles such as healing the antichrist's head wound and calling fire from heaven (maybe a celebration when the antichrist either takes power or is "resurrected"?). He's an effective administrator, carrying out the logistics of how to administer the mark, among other things. But his focus will be religion rather than political power, helping people to meet emotional needs to worship—only not God.

Now back to other "birth pangs."
The Third Jewish Temple in Jerusalem
Another prophecy I didn't formally list is that a Jewish temple must be erected in Jerusalem for the third time in order for some very specific prophecies to be fulfilled during the Tribulation. This prophecy is debated since some Believers say only an altar is required for the "abomination of desolation" as mentioned by both Jesus and Daniel (Matthew 24:15-16, Mark 13:14, Daniel 12:11). An altar has already been constructed in Israel for use in a someday-rebuilt-temple, and that can be instantly installed inside a tent if Jews are ever allowed such spiritual access to the Temple Mount. Right now, Jews are not even permitted to pray in this sacred location. In contrast to the altar-only belief, I believe the antichrist will defile an actual "temple" and that the third temple will be rebuilt and used during the Tribulation.

It's estimated that rebuilding an actual temple will take about two years, so this project could easily begin prior to the Tribulation or after it has begun.

Historical note: Jerusalem's Temple Mount has long been a holy place for Jews and Christians, being on Mount Moriah, where Abraham brought Isaac for the near-sacrifice. Years later, with God's prompting, King David gathered much of the material needed to build a temple, but it was actually David's son Solomon who built the first temple, later destroyed by the Babylonians. The second temple was where Jesus taught, then overturned the moneychanger's tables.

Muslims, too, revere Abraham as the father of their faith, through Hagar's son, Ishmael. There have been various mosques on this site since the 8th century after Muslims conquered the Holy Land in the previous century, just after Muhammed's death. They consider the Temple Mount holy not only out of respect for Abraham but as the place where they believe Muhammad ascended to the Divine Presence for his Miraculous Night Journey around the year 621. It's worthy to note, however, that Muhammad did not designate new holy sites, but rather added his faith to the already existing holy sites of Mecca and the Temple Mount in Jerusalem.

As I mentioned in the brief history of Israel segment, tensions continued between the Muslims and Jews even under the British Mandate, after Britain defeated the Ottomans in 1917. In 1948, when the British handed over the surrounding land for the official rebirth of the nation of Israel, they ceded care for the existing mosque to Jordanian Muslims rather than allowing this plot of land to return to Jewish control.

Almost two decades later, in 1967, Israel decisively won the 6 Day War over territory including the Temple Mount. As a gesture of peace, they allowed the Muslim authority to remain in control of the Mount. The Israeli prime minister vowed no harm would come to this site that's so holy to three faiths (Jews, Christians, Muslims) so protection has been Jewish responsibility even as the Muslims control the mosque itself.

It will take some serious political maneuvering for the Jewish nation to regain control over this area to build the third temple. One source suggested Israel might retake control in exchange for the "two-state solution" that's often touted, i.e. Israel maintaining their own nation while allowing Palestine to become, for the first time in history, an official nation in areas they occupy. In exchange for a separate state, the mosque could be moved to Mecca. However, more than one source says militant Palestinians aren't interested in a two-state solution, preferring to annihilate the Jews and reestablish all of Israel as Palestine. And Israel probably won't believe Palestine will become a peaceful neighbor even if they do become a separate country. On a more promising note, an article in the *Jerusalem Post* suggests some Muslim attitudes are softening toward the Temple Mount, reminding other Muslims that *Mecca* is their most holy spot, and that Jerusalem isn't even mentioned in the Quran. Perhaps God is already at work on the miracle it will take for the third Jerusalem temple to be built.

Although some Muslims deny there ever was a Jewish temple on this spot, there is ample historical proof despite not having had archeological access with Muslims in control. Several stones with inscriptions warning non-Jews against entering the temple have been found on the Temple Mount, as well as a stone that designated a corner as the Trumpeting place to declare Shabbat. Plus, when the Romans destroyed the temple on this site back in 70 AD, they built an arch in Rome displaying how they carried off plunder (specifically a menorah) from the destroyed temple.

And remember that 1927 earthquake I mentioned? Well, it uncovered an ancient Jewish purification pool (a mikveh) at this very spot, dated to the second temple. This discovery came during the British Mandate, but they hid the archeological find in their archives because they thought it would embarrass the Muslims.

Little archeological work has been allowed by Muslims in this area, thus not everyone is entirely certain of the exact location of the former temples on the Temple Mount. They do know the foundation of the first temple served as foundation for the second, so both of the temples stood in the exact same location. Whether that is where the Dome of the Rock stands or other possible spots on the Mount isn't 100% settled. Further archeological investigation will reveal where the temple should be rebuilt.

Today, there is a Temple Movement in Jerusalem preparing to rebuild the temple. As of October of 2022, they've gathered all the furniture and vessels needed for a functional temple, an extensive list of expensive items. In addition to training priests for what they will do after the temple is rebuilt, they've purchased land and are cultivating a Biblical Forest to provide agricultural needs of the temple. Most sacrifices in the Old Testament were plants grown around Israel, in addition to animal sacrifices. Animal sacrifices stopped in 70 AD when the second temple was destroyed, because animals were only to be sacrificed at the Jerusalem temple. (After the temple is rebuilt, prophecy says the antichrist will allow, then disallow, sacrifices in the rebuilt temple. Daniel 9:27, 12:11)

The Temple Movement has also revived what's called Biblical crimson, a special dye used for the garments of the High Priest.

An altar built according to Jewish specifications has also been finished, as noted above, by two activist groups in Israel.

In addition, there is a project to provide a Red Heifer as written in Numbers 19. The ashes of an unblemished red heifer mixed with water are required for purifying Jews for temple service. While the First and Second Temples existed (spanning 1,000 years) only nine red heifers ever met the strict "unblemished" standards for use in this purification process. Jewish tradition (not prophecy) says the tenth heifer will be used by the Messiah or, as Messianic Jews believe, it will be used by Yeshua at His return.

Since there haven't been many red heifers in Israel in modern times (and even the two which were born in recent decades turned out to be blemished), rabbis from the Temple Institute worked with an Israeli cattleman to implant the frozen embryos of Red Angus cattle from North America. Ultimately, offspring from these samples must be perfect red heifers with red hooves; even possessing two hairs of any other color merits disqualification. No wonder only nine heifers met the standard during that 1,000 year span! One video I saw talked about a contingent of rabbis inspecting a herd in Texas, finding no less than ten choices as possible progenitors hopefully capable of producing acceptable offspring. These heifers were shipped to Israel in the fall of 2022, but Scripture says the cattle cannot be transported (they must never have worn a yoke). In September of 2023, the first red heifer from these efforts was born in Israel and is currently being monitored for any blemishes before its third or fourth birthday (the age of sacrifice). Red heifers have returned to Israel, ready to fulfill Numbers 19 requirements and answer Jewish tradition.

Note: The Temple Movement project is a Messianic Jewish (Christian) organization wanting to be prepared for events leading up to Jesus' second coming at any time. Another group, the Temple Institute, consists of orthodox Jews wanting to build the temple for the Messiah, since they don't (yet) believe Jesus already fulfilled that role.

Whether it's the antichrist who aids the rebuilding of the third temple or it's built by other means before then, Israel is more than ready to meet its every need.

One other "birth pang" might be the fact that the Euphrates River is drying. One of the Bowl Judgments in Revelation (16:12) is an angel pouring his bowl on the great river Euphrates. It completely dries up to prepare the way for the kings of the East (thought to be China). The Euphrates must be dry by the second half of the Tribulation when the bowl judgments are unleashed. Either God is already preparing the land around this vital river for the eventual, natural drying, or the river could be purposefully dried by the antichrist using the Euphrates Dam. A recent government report said the Euphrates could naturally run dry by 2040. Of course, climate change predictions are often wrong, so this drying could come about completely by supernatural means. Conclusion: There are so many options for this event that I'm not set on whether or not this current drying is connected to an end times timeline.

. . .

An introduction to the Book of Revelation

I've listened to a number of sermons on the subject given by Skip Heitzig and Jack Hibbs, and what follows is a consolidation of some of the things I've learned from these two wonderful teachers. If you're interested in this subject, I highly recommend finding them on YouTube and listening to their sermons on end times.

As Pastor Skip outlined in one of his sermons, the book of Revelation calls itself prophecy, so we should take it at its word rather than calling it poetry or allegory. It does use symbolic language, as much of the Bible does, but symbolism transcends time and creates a strong mental image for a better emotional connection (just ask any poet!). Revelation also uses first century language when trying to describe modern images, so symbolism was likely a must for those first and subsequent readers.

Revelation also promises a blessing to those who read it. That always impresses me, because so few pastors behind the pulpit talk about it.

Revelation is literally the revelation of Christ, about what John saw at the time of the vision (Jesus in His glorified body), followed by what John saw that was current at the time (the churches and warnings to future churches about possible failings, and perhaps a chronological list of developments for the church in coming years), and lastly what is yet to be (prophetic visions concerning the future of the world, in particular for His chosen people, the Jews). Its main focus is Christ: what He looks like, what He expects of His church, and how He will deal with humanity, specifically Israel, for rebellion.

End times begin with three sets of judgments against a world that's more wicked than ever. The three sets include 7 Seals, 7 Trumpets, and finally, the worst of the worst, the 7 Bowl judgments. I'll list all of them individually a bit later, but here's a peek at the opening from the first set, the first of the 7 seals. This is the beginning of sorrows. In Revelation 6:1-8, we see four horsemen and what they stand for:

- The first horse is white, carrying a leader who offers a short-lived peace. (Antichrist as a man of "peace.")
- The second horse is red, signifying war.
- The third is black, representing famine.
- The fourth horseman rides a pale green horse and represents morbidity (death).

Kicks off to a fun opening, doesn't it? Right off the bat, prophecy tells us a quarter of the earth's population will die, which is way worse than Covid-19. I'm thinking if the church is removed (raptured) just prior to the Tribulation, not only will the world be looking for strong leadership, people will be ripe to do or believe just about anything. War might be a natural outcome after such a situation. If there is any kind of huge war, famines that already occur naturally will worsen because war always impacts farming, transportation, supply, etc. What outcome could there be other than death?

The Gog-Magog War, also known as the Ezekiel War

Let's take a closer look at the war scenario. Some experts believe this second horseman, the one of war, hints at the Gog-Magog war from Ezekiel chapters 38 and 39 where so many specifics of this future war are found. Israel will defend itself against most of the surrounding countries (except for a couple which stay neutral, one being Egypt). Gog, evidently, refers to a title or person, a leader of a northern army, who devises an evil plan. (Ezekiel 38:10)

Many scholars believe Magog to be modern day Russia. Author Joel Rosenberg explains historian Flavius Josephus traced the Scythians back to a son of Japheth who was named Magog. Evidently Scythians were brutal warriors, originating in Iran, who migrated north to the area of Russia. This makes sense if Japheth was Magog's father, since his brothers were Tubal, Gomer and Meschech, who settled modern-day Turkey and also involved in this war. Check the Genesis 10 genealogy for these names. Russians and Turks today would be their descendants, and both countries are against Israel. (Russia is allied with Syria who boycotts Israel, and Turkey recently cut off trade with Israel while the Hamas war continues.)

Magog, or Russia, will partner with Iran (called Persia up until 1935), as well as modern day Turkey (the land of Meschech, Tubal, and Gomer). Cush, as named in ancient times, will also participate. Cush has two possible locations today, Sudan/Ethiopia and southern Iraq. Libya, once called Put (or Phut), will also join the attack against Israel. Iran, Turkey and Libya sympathize with the Palestinians, and technically Iraq has been at war with Israel since 1948 because they never signed a ceasefire. Ethiopia, if that is Cush, is allied with Russia and so without sympathy for Israel. All of this confirms the Bible's predictive element.

According to prophecy, prior to this war, Israel will be living prosperously and at peace in their own nation (like it was just before Hamas attacked in October of 2023). Then Bam! An attack from the north.

An interesting tidbit from Ezekiel refers to Israel's occupants at the time of this war as "gathered from many peoples." This is a perfect description of Israel ever since 1948. Plus, the reason for this Gog-Magog war has never been more fitting: not just to annihilate Israel but also for spoils. Israel has only been prosperous (in modern days) since after it was reestablished in 1948.

The Gog-Magog war is different from the *final* war called Armageddon which is ultimately a war between good and evil at the very end of history as we know it. (Guess which side wins that one?) Certainly there will be no peace in Israel just before Armageddon considering all the terrible things that happen during the seven years leading up to that war. So this Gog-Magog war, *breaking the peace*, isn't likely referring to Armageddon.

As mentioned, I'm assuming this 2023 war in Israel is not the beginning of the Gog-Magog war, even if conditions around the world appear ripe for the war to expand with Israel having very little support. One scholar I listened to said no one except God will come to Israel's aid for the Gog-Magog war. Since we, America, are currently aiding Israel, at least in weaponry, we would have to end that support for this prophecy to apply, according to this teacher.

Also, as of today, no other countries are joining Hamas in their attack, despite Lebanon allowing another terrorist group, Hezbollah, to shoot missiles into Israel. Syria is also allowing mortar fire into Israel, as well as Yemen (Houthis) who are even resorting to piracy against ships they believe belong to Israel. Although Syria and Lebanon are clearly attacks from the north, Russia is not directly involved, and Iran mostly by proxy (supporting Hezbollah). According to a recent article by Pastor Greg Laurie, though, if you wake up to headlines of Russia invading Israel, the Lord's return is imminent.

Although Israel will be under incredible attack during the Gog-Magog war, they will be victorious. For this war, God's intervention will be even more obvious than it was during the 1948, 1967, and 1973 battles—things like a strategic earthquake, flooding, hail, etc., will hasten the end of this particular war unexpectedly, especially if the antichrist steps on the scene.

The ending may be brokered by the antichrist, since the white horseman (antichrist) arrives before the second horseman of war. He must either be newly known or come to prominence as a man of peace to settle this dispute. What a spectacular way to become famous! Brokering a peace deal to end a major war against Israel would be news around the world.

Another consideration is that the antichrist will, for the first three-and-a-half years of the Tribulation, pretend to be a friend to Israel. He might be able to bring together the Palestinians and Jews for peace both sides welcome, and they're able to live side-by-side the way Zionists first imagined Israel could be. Then, suddenly, Israel will be invaded from the north. The Gog-Magog war could take place at any time during the first half of the Tribulation.

Again, the timing of this war is one of those things people find ways to disagree about because no one really knows. We just know it'll happen, because the Bible tells us so.

Another interesting aspect of this war is a specific "clean up" procedure as described in Ezekiel 39. I'm told no other war in the Bible describes how battlefields were cleared. This one is as if a modern day nuclear bomb or biological weapon is involved. According to Scripture, burning the weapons after this war will take seven years to complete. Is this the time it takes to neutralize toxicity from either nuclear or biological weaponry? Or will the burning weapons somehow safely fuel Israeli homes, a "free" energy source lasting seven years?

The dead from this war will be buried in a way never imagined in ancient times when this prophecy was written. Likely because of the care taken, it will take seven months to bury the dead. Human remains will be detected by one team then carefully reburied by another team, after being transported to a valley called Hamon Gog (identified as east of the Dead Sea). One set of professionals will go through the battlefield to identify bones or bodies, another set behind them will do the actual collection for reburial in Hamon Gog. This burial procedure is so extensive a town, perhaps a support station, will be established nearby to monitor the process: the town of Hamonah.

Doesn't this describe how a nuclear disaster, or perhaps a biological weapon, might be carefully handled for the safety of those doing the cleanup, and for the land to recover? Yet these clues were written thousands of years ago. There are varying interpretations, since God allows the birds of the air to devour the flesh of the fallen, and if the bodies are poisoned this suggests they, too, would die which isn't the case. So this is still a question for me. I'm only certain it will take seven months to bury the dead and the procedure for burial will be careful to "cleanse the land."

This war makes sense to happen before or near the outset of the Tribulation because it'll take seven years for the weaponry to burn, using the entire Tribulation period. This also sets off a great revival, because the result of the Gog-Magog war will be a huge spiritual awakening for the Jewish community. (Ezekiel 38) Israelites will see how God miraculously delivers them, and will once again worship Yahweh. It will be a horrible war (as they all are) but this one has a specific outcome: "so that they will know I am Lord." The new Jewish Believers in Christ in Israel will then spread their faith throughout the world for a revival never seen before. They'll be assisted by two witnesses of God, true prophets, who miraculously help spread the Gospel in Jerusalem. Some scholars believe these two witnesses may be Moses and Elijah, Elijah being the prophet who was carried up to heaven in a chariot (2 Kings 2:11) and Moses whose body Satan tried to claim (Jude 9). God has already called Moses and Elijah back into service when they appeared to Jesus and three of the apostles in Matthew 17:3.

I can see already that the material I'm interested in on this topic could take up an entire book all its own, so I'll try to briefly recap some things that will take place during this time.

This timeline, based on my research, is not listed in any strict order. It's difficult to coordinate the many details scattered throughout the Old and New Testaments, especially since there are so many interpretations. If I've left anything out or am ambiguous as to the order, I apologize in advance.

One note here: when Jesus said He is coming "quickly," scholars suggest He was talking about end times, not that He would return quickly after His resurrection. The Tribulation marks the end of the Church Age, so when the Tribulation begins He will indeed "come quickly." Seven years isn't long, unless of course you're living through this period...

Enough said, here goes:

- Rapture (This could happen at any moment. Keep in mind there are various opinions on whether this will

take place just before, during, or at the end of the Tribulation period.)
- Gog-Magog War, a war with northern armies converging to destroy Israel. Scholars differ about when this war will take place: just before the Rapture, just after the Tribulation begins, or closer to the midpoint. Some even suggest it could take place at the end of the Millennium Age. Because of the unique clean-up described in Ezekiel 39, I believe this war will occur just before or near the beginning of the Tribulation.
- Antichrist rises from obscurity, meaning he'll be relatively new on the power stage at the outset of the Tribulation. (That likely leaves out Trump, Newsom, or Elon Musk since they already have notoriety. :-) Three of the ten most powerful nations in the world will hand over power to him relatively quickly.
- Initially, antichrist is revered as a man of peace. He's very charismatic, a world leader everyone admires. Perhaps he's instrumental in protecting Israel, or brokering a deal so Israel can build the third holy temple on the Temple Mount. Or perhaps he's responsible for bringing peace between Israel and the countries that attack during the Gog-Magog war. Antichrist signs a peace treaty with Israel, which he will later break.
- False prophet comes to prominence, who enhances antichrist's appeal and helps expand his power. He's an efficient administrator, but also a renowned spiritual leader.
- Israel is allowed to build the third Jewish temple. Many believe the temple needs to be established for the antichrist to desecrate at the midpoint (three-and-a-half years into the Tribulation).
- At some point in the relatively early period, antichrist may receive what appears to be a mortal head wound (perhaps by an assassination attempt). The false

prophet, in a miraculous way, will heal this wound and revive the antichrist—no doubt spectacularly—for all the world to see.
- False prophet causes "fire from heaven" to appear, perhaps in celebration over antichrist's "resurrection." Drones may be employed for this spectacular sight, or it may be entirely supernatural.
- As a result of Israel's miraculous victory of the Gog-Magog war, a new group of 144,000 Jewish Believers begin to spread the Gospel around the world. This group will be "sealed" by God and miraculously protected from the dangers and evils of this period in time. They will all survive the Tribulation.
- Two witnesses of God also spread the Gospel, and they perform miracles during the first half of the Tribulation. (Revelation 11:3) Many will love their message, but many will hate them. Unlike the sealed witnesses, these two prophets don't survive this seven year period. At the mid-point, they are killed by antichrist and their bodies are left untouched for three-and-a-half days. Since Jewish tradition requires quick burial, this act is basically to dishonor them. Some sources say people blame these two prophets for natural disasters that will have begun to increase in frequency and intensity. Once these prophets are killed, people around the world will celebrate by sending gifts to one another. (Revelation 11:10) Amazon will celebrate with Prime Day sales. (Just kidding; Amazon isn't mentioned in Scripture, even symbolically, as far as I know.) After three-and-a-half days the witnesses will be miraculously resurrected and called up to heaven. (Revelation 11:11-12) This will be seen by the entire world, via the Internet, I'm sure—something impossible to imagine when John wrote Revelation. Their resurrection and removal to heaven will be accompanied by another earthquake. A tenth of

the city of Jerusalem will fall and 7,000 people will die. After this, some people will be so terrified they will finally turn to God. These dramatic events mark the beginning of the second half of the Tribulation, when things get a whole lot worse.

- An angel of God spreads the gospel to the most remote areas of the world. (Wish I could witness that!) Do you see how, even as God is judging the world, He is trying to save as many people as possible?
- Antichrist desecrates the Jewish Temple on the Temple Mount in Jerusalem by having the false prophet erect a statue for all to worship. Somehow this figure will interact with worshippers (likely via AI). Jews, at this point, are called to flee to the mountains.
- The Judgments: 7 Seals, 7 Trumpets, 7 Bowls (Bowls or "vials" being the worst: Woe, woe, woe, unto earth!) There are also 7 Thunders spoken by an angel before the last Trumpet, but John wasn't allowed to write what this angel said so we don't know what they contain.
- Seals 1 through 4 are as mentioned above, the four horses of the Apocalypse. These kick off the Tribulation period.
- Seal #1: Antichrist as depicted on white horse; he comes to prominence as a man of "peace."
- Seal #2: The red horse arrives, signifying that antichrist takes great power. War, perhaps the Gog-Magog war, might not be the only war to break out as fallout from the Rapture. And perhaps it's not only because of war that there will be an increase in killing. After all, if every Christian—the Church—is raptured, Satan won't have any Spirit-filled people getting in his way. People could be desperate and fearful enough to do all kinds of horrible things.
- Seal #3: Black horse: famine, food shortages, disease, inflation. "Oil and wine" not harmed, signifying

affluent people will go on their merry way while the rest of those left behind will basically become slaves: lots of work for money that doesn't buy much.
- Seal #4: Pale green horse: One fourth of the world population will die via war, hunger, pestilence, or death by the "wild beasts" of the earth, beasts in this symbolic language being other kings or leaders aiding the antichrist in mass slaughters. Newly believing Christians will be targeted, but if history teaches us anything, these struggles will likely be to increase sheer power using ideology from politics or religion.
- Seal #5: The martyrs cry out in heaven: *How long will it be to avenge our deaths?* God tells them they must wait for the completion of His plan. (This isn't really a judgment, but is a reflection of what will happen in heaven at the time.)
- Seal #6: A huge earthquake while stars fall from heaven. Even the great and mighty will hide from what seems like the wrath of God, fearing He might come after them next. Yet, somehow, many still refuse to repent. One source I read suggested the stars falling from heaven might be meteor activity, which will only be the first glimpse of that kind.
- Seal #7: Prelude to the next set of judgments: Total silence in heaven, for a half hour. Then an angel with a censer (a container used in religious ceremonies) that's filled with fire throws it to earth, resulting in "noises, thunder, lightning" and another earthquake. One source suggested it might be a supernova accompanying this earthquake. This is the last of the seals.
- The Trumpet judgments likely take place around the middle of the Tribulation.
- Trumpet #1: Hail and fire. One-third of the trees and grass will burn. Wildfires, smoke clouds, environmental disaster. Perhaps the blood-like phenomena associated

with this judgment might be fallout from volcanic activity resulting from the two earthquakes mentioned in the seals, above. These earthquakes, remember, are like the final stages of birth pangs—coming closer together and increasing in severity from what we've experienced before the Tribulation. Would such severe earthquakes start a chain reaction to include volcanic activity as well? Natural minerals and chemicals could cause the smoke to tinge with color, or literal blood could be involved if an eruption is large enough since the smoke would spread everything the blast touches. Think of a super volcano eruption—like Yellowstone, which has the potential to take out entire western cities. There are about 20 known super volcanoes on Earth.

- Trumpet #2: Great "mountain" hits the sea: meaning a giant, burning meteor will kill one-third of all living creatures in the ocean. One-third of all ships on the sea will perish. One-third of the sea becomes "blood" from all the deaths, or perhaps another natural phenomenon like red algae.
- Trumpet #3: Great star burning like a torch hits earth, poisoning rivers and springs. This disaster will poison a third of the fresh water, perhaps exacerbated by nuclear plants close to water sources, causing more death because of bitter (contaminated) water supplies.
- Trumpet #4: One-third of the light from the sun, moon and stars is blocked, dimming the skies (likely as a result of the previous meteors). At the same time, more activity in heaven as recorded in Revelation 8:13 KJV: an angel crying in a loud voice: "Woe, woe, woe, to the inhabiters of earth by reason of the other three voices of the trumpet of the three angels, which are yet to sound!" (Uh-oh . . .)
- Trumpet #5: A star falls and is "given the keys to the abyss" — in other words, what some people describe as

a demon (fallen/cast from heaven) opens an abyss which releases locusts who only attack people without the seal of God on their forehead (those who have given their allegiance to antichrist). These bites, or stings, will be similar to a scorpion bite and cause the people to beg for death but it eludes them. This swarm, or perhaps the symptoms, will last five months. These locusts have extraordinary features and I haven't really come across a strong symbolic interpretation to convince me one way or another. Perhaps they are demons, or perhaps a biological weapon. Years ago, I even read these locusts could be a first century interpretation of what a helicopter might look like, with human pilots and the ability to fly and "sting." Whatever they are, they are destructive. Other than as a protein source for John the Baptist, locusts in the Bible are bad news. These end time locusts do not go after trees, plants or grass, just the people who have not repented. (My advice is to repent!) Smoke accompanies this event, darkening the skies again.

- Trumpet #6: The second woe of the three woes comes in the form of four demonic forces being released from the Euphrates River to kill one-third of mankind. (Remember, one-quarter of mankind is already dead from previous judgments, so now we're up to 58% of the original population being killed.) This trumpet also mentions a 200 million-strong army, and so far I've come across two interpretations for this. One is that they are 200 million demons sent throughout the world to cause one-third of the population to die. Another interpretation is that this will be a literal army of 200 million soldiers, likely from China, to ultimately participate in the final battles of Armageddon. At no time in history has there been a country with the capacity to call to arms an army this

size . . . until now, with China's population well over a billion.
- Trumpet #7: Final woe. Heaven is beginning to rejoice because the end is drawing near. Soon the kingdoms of this world will become kingdoms of the Lord. God's judgment is directed at those who are responsible for killing the martyrs, who continue to rebel against God despite all the supernatural events. This final trumpet involves more lightning, noises, thunder, another earthquake, and great hail (although not as big as the hail that falls during Armageddon, so read on!).
- Bowl Judgments take place toward the end of the Tribulation.
- Bowl #1: Boils. Need I say more? These are "foul and loathsome sores," reserved for those who received the mark of the beast.
- Bowl #2: This bowl is poured out as if blood from a dead man, and every living creature of the sea dies from this poisoning.
- Bowl #3: The rivers and springs turn to blood. God is, either literally or figuratively, giving those on earth the blood of the martyrs. Or, as some end time sites mention (also mentioned by my friend Sherri) this could be red algae, another environmental disaster.
- Bowl #4: The sun will scorch men with great heat. If you've doubted climate change so far, this will be the worst case scenario come true. Or this may be the result of a solar flare. And yet, people still curse God rather than turn to Him.
- Bowl #5: Darkness descends on the "kingdom of the beast," meaning on antichrist's reign. Does this mean the armies that gather at Armageddon will initially rise against antichrist, who might have set up his headquarters in Jerusalem? At this time, victims are still blaspheming God for the pain from their sores. If these

are the same sores meaning "boils" from the first bowl, then these bowl judgments follow quickly one after another.
- Bowl #6: The Euphrates River dries up, preparing the way for the kings of the East (China and other Asian nations). This is in preparation of the final battle that takes place in Israel, with the staging ground at Armageddon. The three unclean spirits mentioned here are the unholy "trinity" of Satan, antichrist and the false prophet. Demonic spirits come from their mouths to persuade other kings of the earth to gather at Armageddon, where, nearby, they eventually will take on no less than God Himself.
- Bowl #7: The greatest and most severe earthquake occurs, worse than any earthquake in the history of this planet, and is very far-reaching. Babylon (in modern day Iraq) which will have gained prominence, now falls. Babylon is the only city named in this catastrophe but we can assume many other cities tumble as well. (For more information on the symbolic significance of Babylon, see Skip Heitzig's book *You Can Understand the Book of Revelation*.) Jerusalem itself is split into three (sources I checked agree this is a reference to Jerusalem, though this "great" city is not specifically named). And finally, the most massive hail ever rains down on earth, each weighing a "talent"—between 75 and 100 pounds. This likely occurs during the battles of Armageddon, because of its placement in Revelation 16.

After reading about so many horrors, contemplating how many people will perish, you may be asking why a supposedly good and loving God would put mankind through such a harrowing end. After all, we're taught He's not willing that any should perish.

God has been patient for thousands of years so far, placing in the Bible and His book of nature every hint we need pointing to a loving Creator. And no matter where we live, He's given us a conscience that senses His morality. He's even sent missionaries around the world and friends to us, those imperfect saints in our lives, to tell us about Him. Yet people continue to reject Him.

The extraordinary events of end times are His last, most dramatic effort to prove to all that He is a supernatural God. All these incredible events point to His Deity. Surely these are the signs and wonders of absolute power over nature. Yet many people still won't repent. Sign after sign of His power continue to be rebuffed. Scripture says people will curse and blaspheme the God displaying this power.

But even during the Tribulation, if anyone repents He will let His Son's blood cover their sins and welcome them into heaven. Those who continue to curse God simply don't want to spend eternity with their Creator.

Warning: 2 Thessalonians talks about a "strong delusion" during the time of the lawless one (antichrist):

> [9]This man will come to do the work of Satan with counterfeit power and signs and miracles. [10]He will use every kind of evil deception to fool those on their way to destruction, because they refuse to love and accept the truth that would save them. [11]So God will cause them to be greatly deceived, and they will believe these lies. [12]Then they will be condemned for enjoying evil rather than believing the truth. 2 Thessalonians 2:9-12 NLT

Many people, myself included, are disturbed by this idea of God "causing" them to be deceived, especially during such desperate times. But reading it in context, it says they've already refused the truth about God; they're *on their way* to destruction because they've rejected God. He knows they wouldn't have turned to Him anyway, at least by faith alone. Would they turn to Him if they knew all of the astonishing activity during this time will be fulfilled prophecies they've been told about in advance (i.e. through this book, for example!)? Would coming to Him take faith, or just common sense at that point? As I've often reminded myself, God set up a *faith*-based system. Seeing before their eyes everything happening in the order it was to happen may have opened eyes that never wanted to be opened toward Him. So He allows them to be deceived by antichrist, and they go on to enjoy evil rather than believing the truth they've already rejected.

Which makes me want to pray even harder for those reading this who won't see the Bible as truth until it's too late.

One last reference, and that's to **Armageddon**, the final battle on Earth. Even as far back as Psalm 2, God has warned us there will eventually be a battle between God and man.

Nearly everyone today has heard of Armageddon, even without having picked up a Bible, thanks to Hollywood. Armageddon is a real place in Israel, also called (Mt.) Megiddo. It's a large area consisting of an archeological site, a popular tourist destination, and pastoral crop land—wide open, perfect as a gathering place for vast armies. After all, this same piece of ground has been used before for war (one source said at least 34 times, another said 200 times if you include ancient wars; just Google wars fought on Israel's Armageddon). Even Napoleon assessed the area as a perfect spot to gather armies.

The ten nations that, at first, cooperate with antichrist during the Tribulation may, in the end, turn on him if Daniel 11 is interpreted correctly. Perhaps the antichrist will headquarter in Jerusalem. Or, perhaps the entire world descends on Israel just because it's Israel, which seems more plausible every day seeing antisemitism rise.

As mentioned above, the Euphrates will dry up, allowing easier access from the East and the North to "trouble the antichrist" (Daniel 11:44). This hints the armies are indeed, at least initially, gathering against him. Who knows, perhaps China's Belt and Road Initiative will come in handy for this march. The Euphrates runs from the foot of Mt. Ararat through Turkey, Syria, Iraq and into the Persian Gulf—all through Muslim territory. If the 200 million-strong army consists of soldiers from China and Asia (and not demons sent to spread support against God), they will likely be allowed passage through these countries for battle on Israeli territory. In a mysterious form of proof that God's Hand is on this land, just look at how central the Jewish people and their homeland have been throughout such a long history of mankind.

The world's combined forces will invade and take into captivity or exile half of Israel. They'll loot, plunder, and ravish women (as happens in every war, including the recent Hamas attack). Ultimately, eventually, this turns to a battle between good and evil, when forces unite to fight God Himself.

This battle will end when Christ appears at the Mount of Olives. Every eye will see Him. **This is Jesus' second coming.** Jesus will return to the same spot from which He ascended forty days after His resurrection. (Acts 1:12)

Historical note and wrapping it up

Prior to 1967, the Mount of Olives was in Jordanian control. But after the Six Day War, Israel gained control. Having the Mount of Olives once again as part of Israel is yet another indicator that the pieces for end times have been falling into place, since Armageddon is actually a staging ground for an invasion of "Israel."

Allow me to highlight yet another archeological miracle. As just stated, Jesus' second coming will take place at the Mount of Olives. The moment His feet touch ground there will be an earthquake. South will separate from the north to create a huge chasm. (Zechariah 14:4)

In 1964, in preparation to build a hotel on the Mount of Olives (now called the Hotel of the Seven Arches) a geographical survey and excavation were done. The original site ended up being relocated, because they found a fault line. After further excavation, they discovered evidence that perfectly describes the earthquake Amos predicted in his book that happened around 750 BC, which Zechariah referenced more than two hundred years later in his. The reason Zechariah mentioned the "Amos" quake? Because he foretold another earthquake would happen at this very site again—when Jesus returns. He tells of how the Mount of Olives will be split from east to west to form a large valley, and half will separate north from south. The fault line they discovered runs east-west, with a north-south offshoot. Current seismic movement (yearly increments) confirm Zechariah's description of what will happen at some point, and the Bible tells us it'll happen when Jesus steps foot on this ground.

After the battle of Armageddon, antichrist and false prophet are thrown into the lake of fire, never to be heard from again, and Satan is pitched into the bottomless pit where he remains for the 1,000 year Millennium period that follows the Tribulation on this present earth. Then Satan is let out one last time to give those born during this age a final choice: choose self and Satan, or God.

After that, Satan is cast into the lake of fire for eternity.

A final judgment will then take place, of those whose names are not written in the Book of Life (unbelievers). They are sent to an eternity based on their choice in life: one without God. Hell is not a party place for cool rebels; it is a place of isolation, darkness, and eternal gnashing of teeth because they could have ended up in heaven instead. Eternal torment is not an understatement.

The final judgment ends, ushering in a new heaven and new earth and an eternity with God Himself as the tabernacle for those who accepted God's love and forgiveness. We have fellowship with Him and with each other—forever!

I can imagine many different reactions to this segment. Some may not have heard about this in much detail, or have varying interpretations of certain prophecies (another opportunity to agree to disagree). Others may think there is more symbolism than a literal future as described. Still others may begin to doubt my sanity and the sanity of others who call themselves Christians and discreetly entertain such fantastical beliefs.

But, if you believe in the reality of a spiritual dimension, perhaps it's not really so fantastical. Read on for evidence of a spiritual dimension, which supports my belief that the Bible is the Word of God.

There are many mysteries throughout Scripture, which is one more reason to believe in its divine inspiration. Certainly prophecy is one of them!

Personal Testimony & the Spiritual Realm

Now we come to the personal stuff. Depending on which apologist you're listening to, the value of personal testimonies ranges from marginal to profound. Marginal, because personal experiences can be impactful on the person and perhaps their friends and family, but beyond that can be pretty easily dismissed. "I'm glad it's working for you, but it's not for me," is a common argument against the power of personal testimonies.

On the other hand, personal testimonies can't be disputed if the person sharing their unique experience is corroborated by an apparent life change.

I think it can be accurately stated that the more dramatic or emotional a personal testimony might be, the more often it'll be used when talking to others. I guess that's why my husband and I rarely bring up our personal testimonies. Although they were certainly impactful, they're not very interesting to anyone but us. My husband came to faith by himself (well, not apart from the Holy Spirit's involvement!). He followed a sincere quest for truth about the origins of this planet and of life and whether or not God really had anything to do with it. He was also struck by the language describing God as the Great I AM, indicating an eternal God outside of time. His is what I call an intellectual's journey to faith.

My testimony includes a person-to-person introduction to the gospel, coming through my brother Mark. My brother had gone off to college but came back filled with the Holy Spirit. I was very young, just in middle school, but even back then I was writing stories. In a timing incident orchestrated by God, I happened to have a character in one of my manuscripts who liked quoting phrases of wisdom. Where was I, as the twelve-year-old creator of this character, going to find wisdom? Not in myself or my limited experiences. So I pulled out our rarely-read family Bible, a big, old volume that mostly served as an ancestry record with pages our mother had filled in. Mark was so surprised to find me bent over this Book that he immediately shared the gospel. I liked hearing about a God who was more personal than what I'd been taught at Friday catechism classes. That began my earnest pursuit to know more about Him.

Here I am, closer to the end of my life than the beginning, and I must say I haven't spent the interim years as wisely as I could have. But I do have a nugget of wisdom: God really did change my life, because even though I've disappointed Him many times over, He never gave up on me. All through my lukewarm and downright cold years of my adult youth, I always sensed His presence in my life. And I learned the secret of a happy life: when my choices align with the wisdom God sets out in His Word, a happy life follows—even amid the heartaches of living in a fallen world.

Neil and I are living proof that a life-changing testimony isn't always found on a road to Damascus or with a bolt of lightning. My faith has grown over time, like deepening relationships do, as God's love—found by getting to know Him better—feeds my love for Him.

I'll include in this section something I'll only talk about briefly. It's such a big subject entire books have been written about it, but I won't do more than touch on it. It's suffering.

Why would a good God allow so much suffering?

When I'm confronted with this, all I can say is:

- We live in a fallen world where things like disease, decay and evil exist. We won't see "perfect" until we get to heaven.
- God set up a faith-based system, so suffering appears random.
- We have free will.

First, a note about free will. I'm aware some people don't believe human beings have free will, that we are products of evolution, hard-wired in our finite, matter-only brains. But this atheistic view doesn't make sense to me largely because of what this chapter is all about—experiential, spiritual testimonies. How do you explain any spiritual experience, such as following a nudge from the Holy Spirit to do something for a specific person only to learn that nudge was exactly what that person needed? How do you explain this need to worship, a universal experience, except that God put this need in us as an invitation to get to know Him? How do you explain unexplainable near death experiences or documented miracles? There are just too many spiritual encounters, experienced by too many people around the world and throughout history, for me to discount the existence of a spiritual dimension, including our souls having free will.

Back to suffering. I recall writing an essay published many years ago that talked about my "survivor's blood" and how my family members, like so many others, aren't strangers to suffering. My grandmother lived long enough to bury three of her four children, one of whom was her only daughter, who lived only a few years. My dad suffered more than three years as a prisoner of the Japanese in WWII, under the most brutal conditions you can imagine. I lost a sister to a progressive disease combination of diabetes and cirrhosis. Even now, we have a brother and sister-in-law who have been the caregivers to their medically fragile son for over two decades, an older sister shut-in with severe Parkinson's and a brother with a rare skin disorder called PRP that might very well last the rest of his life.

Finally, as you probably know, (or if you've read my book *The Oak Leaves*) when my son was just over a year old, he was diagnosed with Fragile X Syndrome. It's a spectrum disorder, where some patients function pretty well and others ... not so well. Basically, my son is stuck at about a two-and-a-half year functionality level. Unless they come up with some kind of miraculous treatment, he will have these limitations for the rest of his life. With an expected normal life span he will outlive my husband and me.

When we received this life-changing diagnosis, one of the first questions I asked was "Is God really good?" If so, why did He allow this to happen? Why deprive this sweet little boy a normal, productive life?

After nearly three decades of parenting a two-and-a-half year old I may not have many answers, but I do know my definition of a "good" God wasn't very clear. Of course He's good! I just have to look out my window to see the gifts He's put out there for us to enjoy: the seasons, the colors, the beauty and incredible variety in nature. Fine-tuning, as we looked at in the science segment, proves life is a wondrous miracle. Every day I open the blinds in our bedroom and as I see the beauty of nature I think to myself: I get to live here! I can't even count all the blessings I've had in my life, not the least of which are all my children, including my two non-Fragile X children and their spouses. My disabled son may have given us special challenges these past three decades, but I realize God's hand was in it. My husband and I not only handled those challenges (at times better than at others) but we know our son has always been safe under our care. Who better to allow such a challenge than those who can handle it?

In any case, God didn't create disease any more than He created evil. He wants to put an end to all disease and evil—even though it's our free will that ushered in such things to begin with. That's what the Bible is all about, how God created us, paved a way for Christ so if we choose, we can ask Him to blot out our sins with His shed blood, and let the Holy Spirit guide us through everyday life until we join Him for everlasting fellowship in heaven.

God isn't just a "good" God. (Mark 10:18) He is also perfect. None of us can live up to perfect. Some of us do more than just fall a bit short. We aim for true rebellion. That's how evil was born, and disease is a byproduct. Not that sickness or suffering is a result of any person's specific sin, but sickness and evil are a result of free will for all of us (and angels' too) since the beginning of creation.

God can't shield His children from the decaying world around us and still maintain His faith-based system. If all it took to avoid anything bad happening to us was to become a Christian, then people would jump onto the "faith" wagon just to avoid the consequences of evil. No actual faith would be required, just join Christianity out of pure self-preservation. So of course we can't be spared.

Besides, God can and does use our suffering for good. Here's a list of ways God uses suffering for our benefit, as originally told by Pastor Jeff Griffin of Compass Church in Naperville, IL.:

- 2 Peter 3:9 **Salvation**. Why doesn't God bring us to heaven right now, where there is no more suffering? Because not all would be saved. As we await the end of our suffering, God is bringing more people to salvation.
- Romans 5:3-4 **Sanctification**. This is a fancy word that means in our suffering, we can grow in endurance, character, and hope.
- Romans 8:1-7 **Bonding**. Knowing Jesus also suffered, we realize He understands our suffering. He was rejected by the very people He created to love. We have a shared experience, which deepens our bond with Him.
- 2 Corinthians 1:4 **Comforting**. Those who suffer and are ministered to by God can comfort others who suffer, because of their understanding of suffering.
- 1 Peter 1:6-7 **Evidence**. How Christians endure and are ultimately victorious over suffering is evidence of God's involvement in our lives.

- John 9:3 **Display**. God's power can be seen in those who suffer as they trust God to help them through their suffering.
- 2 Corinthians 1:9 **Reliance**. In the midst of suffering, we often feel closer to God by trusting Him rather than ourselves.
- Psalm 119:67 **Correction**. Unhealthy behavior can sometimes be redirected by suffering.

The good news is our suffering has an expiration date. The trajectory of life isn't womb to tomb. It's womb to eternity. Someday this life will be replaced by a reality that's infinitely longer, without pain, difficulties, or even tears.

And the best news, at least for me? In heaven, I'll get to have a real, honest-to-goodness conversation with my currently non-verbal son!

Evidence for a spiritual realm

Before I go on, I want to address the elephant in this particular room. As I mentioned elsewhere, the Bible would receive far more academic acceptance without "all that supernatural stuff." If it were just historical, if Jesus were just a good and kind martyred historical figure, or if Scripture only recounted an accurate order of creation as science understands it today but without a "creator," there would be no controversy.

Which leads me to an obvious question for those struggling to believe in God: is there room in your mind for the spiritual realm? (2 Corinthians 4:18) Room for a God who actually spoke to Christianity's patriarchs (Exodus 33:1), a God who raised Jesus from the dead (Romans 10:9), a God whose Hand guided and guarded the information Christians treasure today as His Word? (2 Timothy 3:16)

As Josh McDowell says, we come to every choice in life with presuppositions. If a person presupposes there is no spiritual realm, then whatever I write here will be discounted before the words are even read. (1 Corinthians 2:14) Which is why I'm taking a pause, to acknowledge that fact and ask for consideration of the following in spite of deep skepticism. Without miracles, after all, there would be no case for Christianity.

For me, this topic reminds me of something our church pastor, Lisa Seaton, said during one of her wonderful sermons: our lives aren't as physical beings having a spiritual experience, we're spiritual beings having a physical experience.

Today's headlines often include incredible events, such as UFOs or UAPs as they're called now (Unidentified Ariel Phenomena or Unidentified Atmospheric Phenomena, take your pick). It's hard to doubt *something* is flying in our skies, whether they're enemy drones, falling debris from space (heaven knows there's lots of that, since I personally saw flaming debris fall into my neighbor's yard this year), or a UAP.

I'm not particularly passionate either for or against actual aliens. I guess if God created other forms of life, I wouldn't expect that information to invalidate my trust in God or the Word He gave us for this one.

However, my belief in flying objects leans more in favor of the spiritual realm surrounding this Earth than actual aliens from other planets or solar systems.

Hugh Ross (reasons.org) explains that most UFOs/UAPs have a natural validation. However, there is a small percentage that really do defy explanation. There are reports from pilots who see something moving at a speed too fast for the sudden turns they make, or at least too fast for any human to survive a turn at that speed. Evidently when our fastest aircraft makes a turn, it takes quite a distance to complete. Some of the UAPs being seen worldwide describe sharp, sudden changes in direction, 180º turns.

There are also sightings of something falling to the ground, leaving evidence of a burned crater, yet leaving absolutely no physical debris at the site. No singed space craft, no trace or "alien" chemicals found in the ground. Nothing, except evidence that something landed.

More descriptions of UAPs include flying above water, descending below the water without a splash, then resurfacing—all at incredible speed, as if the water had no effect. I even heard one story where multiple (human-operated) planes were flying together and sensors suddenly sounded a warning: one of their aircraft was about to collide with another flying object. Miraculously, the UAP passed through the plane with nothing more than blips on their radar showing what should have been a collision, but wasn't.

Recently Congress held a hearing to interview several witnesses, credentialed, serious-minded people, under oath, about UAPs. It proved we're living in extraordinary times, when in the past something like this would have been viewed as crazy. I don't doubt the witness's sincerity; I do question the source of these sightings.

I believe they're proof of a spiritual world. Almost all UFO experiences are negative: unpleasant or frightening interaction, even in some cases unwilling experimentation or abduction, encounters often followed by terrifying dreams. Because of this, Hugh Ross believes, as I do, that these encounters are with demons. The Bible speaks of our battles against the spiritual forces of heavenly places. (Ephesians 6:12) When Dr. Ross researched the phenomena of someone having repeat occurrences with UFOs, he found many of those people had been dabbling and/or were exposed to increased occult activity. In other words, some cases invited demonic activity. Satan likes to divert our faith, so we might finally take God off the table as the originator of life.

The Bible says in end times there will be an increase in deceptive spirits and demons (1 Timothy 4:1) and this increase in activity could be the fulfillment of this prophecy.

Speaking of demonic activity, that's another area of evidence for a spiritual realm. 1 Peter 5:8 warns specifically of the devil prowling and looking for someone to devour, and he targeted my friend

Sarah. Sarah participated in witchcraft when she was a teenager. Her "spirit guide" seemed to comfort her at first, but ultimately it led her to a suicide attempt. Her experience is certainly evidence for the spiritual realm. Thank God she went off to college, where God arranged for her to have Christian roommates who invited her to a sermon God used to bring her to faith and knowledge of her importance to Him.

The dying process also offers ample evidence for a spiritual realm. Jesus told us if we believe in Him we will never die (John 11:26), obviously suggesting life goes on after our physical death. When I was a child, I had an Aunt Josephine who nearly died during a surgical procedure. She survived, living to tell how she went to a place so beautiful she couldn't really describe it. She saw flowers and colors unlike anything here on earth. She'd described it with such peace the memory is still with me today.

I have two immediate family members who also proved to me there is a spiritual realm. First, my sister Laura. Due to illness, she knew she was dying for several months before it happened. She was an incredible example of faith, peace and kindness to everyone who took care of her.

One morning, I came in to her room and she said she needed to talk to our brother Mark. She didn't seem troubled, just eager to tell him something. As you know from this book, Mark is a pastor. Laura wanted to explain to him about the mistake she'd been making through her dying process. I asked what mistake she could possibly have made, because as I said she was a wonderful example of kindness and gratitude to the entire staff during her hospice care. She told me she'd been looking at death the wrong way. Apparently she had a spiritual experience that made her realize she'd been concentrating too much on what was happening to her. Prior to this experience, on occasion during her last few months, she'd been frustrated to wake up in the morning, wondering why God hadn't taken her during the night. But on that morning, she told me, it's *all* about God. All about God, she repeated more than once. She was miraculously peaceful after this spiritual revelation—an experience that had been a conversation *with* God, not just a prayer *to* Him. Within a few weeks, she died. Peacefully.

My other experience is from my dad. He had a twenty-four-hour home health caregiver, Alex, who was from the Philippines. Alex and Dad got along really well, because my dad had fought alongside the Philippine forces against the Japanese in the Second World War. That meant a lot to Alex who, although a lot younger, expressed gratitude for my dad's service to defend Alex's homeland. Alex didn't hesitate to let my dad know he was proud to be his caregiver because my dad was a hero to him.

One day near the end of his life, my dad told Alex that his mother had visited him. Since my dad was in his early eighties at the time, his mom had passed away a number of years prior. Alex asked my dad if she'd spoken, and my dad said she told him it was time for him to come home. Had she visited to let him know she would be his heavenly escort, as is so common in near death experiences? Besides that, why use the phrase "come home"? My dad was very private about his faith and I do not ever recall him saying he'd someday "go home" to heaven. My dad died not long after that experience, and I have little doubt his mom met his soul as he departed his earthly body.

Alex later told our family these kinds of experiences from his hospice patients aren't uncommon.

The following brief accounts are from people I or a family member know personally and absolutely trust their integrity.

I worked with a woman whose husband, a pastor, had died at her side some years before I met her. He had been ill, but she described him during his last moments on Earth as sitting up in bed, reaching out his arms as if to embrace someone greeting him from above, then dying—all in a matter of moments.

The other experience comes from a family member who used to babysit for a sister and brother when they were kids. David grew up to love the Lord! However, as he approached his fortifourth birthday he was diagnosed with pancreatic cancer. Near the end of his life, his sister Jackie, also a Believer, knew she needed to say a difficult goodbye. So she wrote a letter to express how much she loved him and how grateful she'd always been to have him as her older brother. She took the letter to his bedside, knowing by this time he was too weak and sleepy to have much of a conversation. She assured him it would take less than five minutes for her to read her letter, and hoped he could stay awake. Included in this goodbye she shared something she'd never told him, about her multiple miscarriages. She told him the names of each of her babies she'd given as a tribute to their very real existence. Naming them was a detail she hadn't shared with anyone else, not even her husband.

When Jackie finished reading, her brother smiled and appeared happier and more alert than he'd been for a while. He asked her who had told her to write that letter. The question surprised Jackie, and she said no one had told her, she'd just written what was on her heart. No, her brother said, your daughter Emma told you to write it. She looks just like you, by the way.

Jackie, who had likely hoped to bring comfort to her brother by saying he would soon be meeting her children already in heaven, was the one who was astoundingly comforted. He seemed to have already met at least one of her children!

I did some general reading about near death experiences (NDEs), only trusting studies rather than individuals I didn't know. Professional sources checked motives of those telling such stories as well as scientific data like medical records testifying that brain activity actually ceased for these individuals before they were revived. The testimonies I researched didn't result in anyone's fame or gaining a fortune; in fact, several people only talked about it after their doctor asked if anything "unusual" happened during their critical health challenge. Many were reluctant to share their experience, at least with medical personnel, for fear of being thought of as crazy. It's an interesting topic if you have time to go into it deeper, but it's probably best to stick to professional studies rather than individuals on social media who might have ulterior motives in telling amazing stories.

One experience I read about described a woman who was blind

from birth. During surgery she "died" on the table. She, like so many others who experienced such a thing, described in detail what went on outside of her unconscious body. She could see, for the first time since she'd been born blind, what her doctor looked like. What the room looked like, and methods they used on her body in order to save her. When she was revived, her blindness was still there, but she told the doctor all the things she'd seen through the perfect vision of her soul.

Another woman, also blind from birth, reported seeing two of her lifelong friends for the first time. They, too, had been blind, but they'd both died at some point prior to this. Although this woman had never seen them because of her blindness, she was able to describe their features in detail after her NDE.

When I looked up other accounts of restored sight during an NDE, I also found accounts of "beyond perfect vision"—like my aunt, who saw colors she'd never seen before.

Another account is of a tragic car wreck involving a mother and her two sons. The mother died at the scene but the two boys were still alive and taken to separate hospitals. One of the boys revived briefly, completely at peace, and told the doctor that he was all right because his mother and brother were waiting for him. Then he died. The doctor went to the nursing station afterward, where they'd received a call from the other hospital. The brother had died minutes before the little boy had regained consciousness, only neither the doctor nor the boy could have known except through this spiritual experience.

Another report is of a woman who was met by several relatives at her near death experience. She recognized everyone, including a dear cousin whom she hadn't seen recently. She was surprised to see this cousin there, since she wasn't dead. Later, after being revived and while recovering, her husband told her he had some bad news. Her cousin had died the previous week, only he'd just found out. It was the cousin she'd seen in heaven.

Lee Strobel, in his book *A Case for Heaven*, recounted an Oxford study which surveyed 17,000 people who had experienced

NDEs. Ten percent reported seeing someone on the other side who wasn't supposed to be there—people who had died without the person experiencing the NDE knowing in advance.

Besides that, their descriptions of what went on around them at the time of departure from their body were 440% more accurate than any naturalistic explanation—i.e. if a person without an NDE described what they might have expected the operating room to look like, what the doctors were doing, those with an out-of-body experience were that much more accurate. Expectations don't explain these experiences.

Patients brought back from this kind of experience recall vivid details of the resuscitation process, including sounds. One case described how the doctors talked about having difficulty finding the woman's very small veins. Was this because of faulty anesthesia? You decide.

A recap of nearly all the experiences I read about from around the world have striking similarities, regardless of culture. Children having these experiences are comforted about where they're going, sometimes even resulting in a new faith even if their household hadn't previously exposed them to such ideas. Some report going to a beautiful place they're told is heaven, and they will be coming there soon. A common result for children is no more fear of death.

Many people, young or old, see angelic beings. One child who had such an experience told his parents about the angels. The parent made the mistake of trying to support him by saying they, too, had seen the angels. But when the parent described the angels as having wings, the child told this parent not to lie. They absolutely did not have wings. Wings on angels are a common assumption in our Western culture, when in fact the Bible tells us only certain heavenly beings have such things: Cherubim in Hebrews 9:5 and Psalm 18:10, Seraphim in Isaiah 6:2.

There is often a tunnel, or darkness with light in the distance, the feeling that the person is outside of time and distance (meaning they feel like they're traveling, but it doesn't take the normal time to move from one spot to another), there seems to be a destination, and they're often greeted by familiar people. The experience is most often (though not always) accompanied by peace. Finally, there is normally a recognition that they've come into God's presence and a feeling of love. God, from some cultures, may not be recognized as Jesus the way He is among Christians, but nonetheless even among cultures with many gods there is a recognition of "a" (singular) Godlike presence.

As Lee Strobel asks: are NDEs wishful thinking, the brain's last-ditch effort to stay alive? Mental illness? Chemicals in the brain that spur memories? A brain spasm? If they're wishful thinking, why do even atheists (without any expectation of an afterlife) experience them as well as those with faith? Why would wishful thinking sometimes produce a frightening experience? About one in five NDEs are reported as being demonic in nature, or a visit to hell, often resulting in a change of life afterward. If NDEs are spurred by chemicals, why is there such a feeling of completeness associated with them? Not drug-induced confusion or chaos associated with random things either in their life or around them, but an orderly, peaceful, completed experience including conversations with others?

Why are so many "experiencers" more peaceful, less fearful of death, and less materialistic after something like this? (At least those with positive NDEs!)

And as for brain activity, NDE studies these days include documentation that the brain ceased working. As for mental illness, there are too many accurate descriptions of things outside the body at the time for this to explain what happened.

These experiences aren't described as a dream, which more often than not end abruptly. These experiences seemed to have resolution, often a review of life, often a choice of whether or not to stay or go back, with some kind of conversation that isn't cut off but allowed to conclude. Hallucinations, like dreams, usually end abruptly, without the closure experienced in NDEs. In short, the place they go feels "more real than real."

Also according to Strobel's book, NDEs are more common

than we think. Approximately four to six percent of the population have lived to tell about such an experience, perhaps in part because doctors are better able to revive people in recent years. In fact, eighty percent of those under hospice care go through some form of this, often not a full-blown NDE, but including visits from deceased relatives as described by my father and others, or new spiritual insight like my sister's.

One last comment on this. Some agree NDEs are connected to the spiritual realm, but could be demonic. I've read several accounts which offer assurances to the person that everyone ends up in heaven, or one experience confirming a gut feeling if they'd stayed longer they would have been reincarnated. One man even described how he'd been greeted by rude, insulting creatures who escorted him on some sort of descent. The longer he was there, the uglier these creatures became, and the rudeness turned to cruelty. His NDE was a visit to hell. It frightened the man so much he turned his life around. He sought the truth the Bible offers and ended up becoming a pastor.

Others, perhaps with more positive experiences, were so profoundly impacted they wanted to recreate conditions to feel it all again. Some tried drugs. Some visited spiritualists and dabbled in the occult. Some investigated mystical religions. If people don't seek and verify truth, or are fooled like my friend Sarah was by a spiritual "guide," it will take them farther away rather than toward the loving, personal God of the Bible with its proven truths. They are playing with demonic forces and will open themselves up to deception. The Bible warns us not to dabble with divination: 2 Kings 21:6 and Leviticus 19:31 and 20:6.

In any case, NDEs are common enough to strongly suggest we do have a soul and consciousness after death. We are, in fact, spiritual beings having a physical experience!

God's Involvement in American History Proves a Spiritual Realm—investigated because, as you know, I love history!

It seems in recent years we've been hearing more about America's failings than strengths. Obviously, like any other era in history, our own is filled with highs and lows. The original explorers, then colonists, then waves of immigrants, brought new diseases to the indigenous First Nation population. The wars that followed between the British/American army and Native Americans were as terrible as any other war of conquest in man's often ugly history. We have the stains of slavery, of prejudice and classism, of sexism, and all the other shortcomings common to human behavior which fall short of God's expectations. (Thus the need for a savior!)

However, this is a nation blessed by God. We've sent our young soldiers into battle for freedom, not only on our own soil but overseas. As the saying goes, we came to the aid of other countries asking nothing in return but the soil upon which to bury our dead.

Many years ago, Michael Medved, a conservative radio host, presented a program about God's Hand on American History. I was so interested in the subject at the time that I purchased his CDs. Recently I re-listened to them. Yep, CDs are still good if you have technology old enough to play such things. The recordings reminded me there are too many extraordinary moments in America's history for all of them to be "coincidence." Here are a few:

Squanto

Tisquantum, better known as Squanto, is the Patuxet Indian who was lured into a slave ship by a "worthless fellow of our nation" (England). Squanto and about twenty other young Native Americans were taken by force to Spain where their captors intended to sell them. History is a little fuzzy if or how long Squanto was a slave. Some stories about his rescue include help from a group of Spanish Friars, but evidently that story isn't corroborated by historical journals piecing together Squanto's experiences.

So, Squanto escaped Spain and made his way to England where

he learned to speak English. There, he worked in a shipyard until he was offered a position aboard a ship bound for Newfoundland. The captain and crew were traders who traveled along the North American coast as far south as Massachusetts. They knew Squanto would be invaluable as a translator with Native Americans. This was Squanto's ticket home.

However, while Squanto had been overseas, disease had wiped out Squanto's tribe. Only by God's Hand was Squanto spared this fate, even through such a horrible experience as being taken captive and the terrible tragedy of losing his tribe. He ended up moving back to the land of his childhood anyway, and eventually was introduced to the struggling pilgrims by another Indian named Samoset. Because of Squanto's fluent English and ease with the colonists, he was able to teach the pilgrims how to live off the land. They likely wouldn't have survived the harsh winters without Squanto's help, and Squanto wouldn't have been there to help them had not God temporarily removed him from his homeland.

George Washington
On July 9, 1755, George Washington fought as a Colonel in the French and Indian War at The Battle of the Monongahela. Washington was a tall man, over six feet, so between that, his horse, his red trousers, red lapels and red vest of a British colonial army colonel's uniform, he was quite a target. He'd also just gotten over a terrible bout with dysentery, and one source I read said this would have caused him to sit up even straighter to lessen any lingering pain. During this particular battle, two horses were killed beneath him. Not only that, as Washington wrote in a letter to his brother afterward, he found four bullet holes in his jacket, all of which miraculously did him no harm. As one Shawnee Indian later bragged, he never missed his target but had shot at the tall man on the horse who wasn't harmed. Evidently others from his tribe had targeted Washington as well, *eleven* times, until they gave up under the belief he was being protected by the Great Spirit.

Say what you will about Washington, whether he was a Deist or Christian or otherwise, he was mostly private about whatever faith he did have. But his Episcopal church attendance, being a vestryman and church warden, all suggest he was a bit more involved in the traditional Christian beliefs common to his day. His nephew is even said to have seen him on his knees with an open Bible before him. History also records Washington's advice to soldiers who swore and gambled that it was "unseemly" to ask God's favor on their war efforts if they were constantly insulting Him with their behavior. That seems to indicate belief in a more personal God.

Christian? Or Deist? I guess we'll find out when we see him in heaven. Or not. What matters here is that God protected Washington, not only through this battle but through numerous health issues including smallpox, tuberculosis and malaria because he would be instrumental in the founding of this country.

God's Material Blessings on America

The timing of the Gold Rush suggests God wanted California in America's hands. On February 2, 1848 the US and Mexico were finally ready to sign a treaty ending the Mexican-American War. Mexico had to hand over California, Nevada, Utah, New Mexico, most of Arizona and Colorado, parts of Oklahoma, Kansas and Wyoming and Texas. For this land, Mexico received fifteen million dollars, and the US government agreed to pay the debts American citizens were owed by the Mexican government. Plus, the US agreed to monitor the border, protect the land and civil rights of Mexicans living in these territories, and be responsible for future arbitration between the two countries regarding the treaty. Judge for yourself whether this is a reasonable settlement between the winning and losing side of yet another historical war.

On January 24, 1848, just days before this treaty had been signed, gold was discovered at Sutter's Mill. Communication being what it was at the time, word hadn't yet spread. How much more difficult and expensive might the treaty have been had such natural resources been known? Would the war even have ended? The Gold Rush not only started a great migration of Americans westward, it brought in a staggering amount of wealth.

Ever heard of William Seward?

In 1865, a guy named William Seward was President Lincoln's Secretary of State. In early April 1865, he was involved in a carriage accident when one of the horses acted up and Seward was thrown to the ground. He was seriously wounded with a broken arm and facial abrasions. He also almost drowned in his own blood from a broken jaw. But Seward survived and was at home recuperating on that fateful night Booth shot Seward's boss at Ford's theater.

Evidently this same group of assassins had also targeted Seward because of his very pro-Union ideology. This was the Civil War era, after all, and loyalties sparked deep emotion.

One of the assassins showed up at Seward's door. He claimed to have a delivery from Seward's doctor and the medicine needed to be given directly to the patient. They let him in, but he was stopped upstairs by Seward's son Frederick (then the Assistant Secretary of State). Frederick refused to tell the man which room housed his father, so the man pulled out a gun and fired at close range. It misfired. He then pistol-whipped Frederick, who went out cold.

Just then Seward's daughter emerged from her father's room. The man then knew where to find the patient, and he first attacked Seward's nurse then Seward himself. This time the assailant used a knife since his gun was no good. Four times the man's knife missed its target. Why? Because the large metal jaw brace used for Seward's recovery from his carriage accident got in the way.

Two years later, Seward, still the Secretary of State, purchased Alaska. You've probably heard of Seward, after all, if you were taught about Seward's Folly. Only this purchase not only brought in the Alaskan gold rush, it also played an important role as our "guardian of the north" during the Cold War.

Oh, and Seward's expansionist ideology later insured America acquired a little island called Midway, which is the place of another miracle I'll mention in a moment.

God's Discipline?
Did I mention that God's Hand sometimes delivers discipline? Well, according to Medved, he believes the Civil War might have been a punishment for our sin of slavery. After all, other countries put an end to this abomination without turning on each other. Yet our war between the states resulted in the greatest number of American deaths from any war in our history.

Why? Perhaps because no other country stated on their founding documents that "all men are created equal." Obviously God took those first documents seriously, and allowed the bloodiest war on our soil to fix that wrong.

The Battle of Midway
I'll finish this history reminiscence with an abbreviated version of an "improbable" victory. While Michael Medved's recording inspired this segment, most of the following information on the battle is from an article by Craig L. Symonds titled *Miracle Men*, published in the February 2012 issue of *World War II Magazine*. This battle has inspired multiple books and movies, and what I've included here is just a glimpse into one angle. My apologies for all of the other action I've had to leave out due to space.

The island (technically an atoll) of Midway is located eleven hundred miles northwest of Hawaii, or "midway" between San Francisco and Tokyo. It's actually part of the Hawaiian Islands but has never officially been included in that state. Back in the mid-1800s, an American ship's captain came across the island and our aforementioned Secretary of State Seward, with his expansionist ideology and dreams of trading with China, decided to officially claim this uninhabited spot for America. Unlike Alaska, there was no gold, just Gooney Birds and their poop, which was a different sort of gold Seward recognized as a valuable ingredient for gunpowder and fertilizer. Best of all, something Seward couldn't have guessed, it turned out to be a strategic spot for our navy in the Second World War.

Picture this: Pearl Harbor, December 1941. The attack on our Hawaiian naval base proved naval battles had progressed from ship-to-ship warfare to battles in the sky, demanding the need for aircraft carriers. On the day of that attack, two of our Pacific Fleet aircraft carriers stationed at Pearl Harbor were at sea on maneuvers, hundreds of miles away. In addition, the Yorktown was destined for the Pacific, but was still in Virginia. What a coincidence these three important ships weren't docked at Pearl Harbor! Or maybe it was the Hand of God. Despite the devastating human loss and crippling destruction of other ships and equipment, we didn't lose any of our Pacific aircraft carriers.

Pearl Harbor was attacked on December 7, 1941 (a day that will live in infamy...). A short time later, in early 1942, our code breakers in Hawaii learned the Japanese were planning another attack for either late May or early June of that year on "AF," soon learned to be Midway. The Japanese wanted to use Midway as a launching pad closer to the US, so they could reign supreme in the Pacific.

Most of the attention from Washington DC at this time was aimed at fighting Hitler. There had even been an order to "avoid decisive action" in the Pacific so our armed forces could concentrate on the European cause. There was some discussion about hiding the remaining aircraft carriers and even letting Midway fall. Reclaim it once our Navy had a chance to rebuild from the December attack, allowing an easier, decisive win then. Since the Japanese had a huge, largely successful fleet and superior aircraft in their Kido Butai, or mobile strike force, it seemed our side didn't have much of a chance.

But of course our Navy developed a plan to defend Midway, starting with reinforcing the atoll. As mentioned, our Pacific Fleet still had three aircraft carriers after the Pearl Harbor attack: the Lexington, Enterprise and Yorktown. But the Japanese sunk the Lexington that May during the Battle of the Coral Sea, a battle both sides claim as victories. This battle also crippled the Yorktown, which the Japanese claimed it sank. However, the ship lapped its way to Hawaii, where round-the-clock crews did a miraculous job getting this important ship back into service in time to help defend Midway. Our side also had a new ship, the Hornet, giving us four surfaces for aircraft, including Midway itself. This matched the four aircraft carriers expected to be used by Japan's Kido Butai on its way.

Japan planned a three-tiered attack on Midway: an air attack early in the day, followed by a land invasion, then the superior Japanese navy would crush any expected US reinforcements.

On the day of the expected attack, our carriers met 325 miles north of Midway, hidden from the Japanese scouts heading that way—not long before two Japanese carriers and two battleships were spotted one hundred seventy miles to their south, releasing the first aerial attack. Although they did significant damage, they didn't hit Midway's runways. It's likely they were ordered not to hit them so they'd still be of use once the Japanese took over.

But as much damage as they wrought, the lead Japanese pilot said a second aerial attack would be necessary before Midway was a "softer" landing for their second phase. Their planes returned to their carriers for refueling and reloading. After learning about the American aircraft carriers in the vicinity, the Japanese planes were rearmed with torpedos, a procedure which took more time than just refueling and rearming with bombs.

Meanwhile, our aircraft carrier Enterprise prepared our planes for an aerial attack against the Japanese vessels, thinking they already knew the strike force's location. Because the planes carried one-thousand-pound bombs they needed the full deck to take off, so maneuvering other planes from the huge hangar below into place on top took more time. Mechanical problems caused delays, but after the dive bombers were ready, more mechanical problems with at least one of the torpedo bombers accounted for another delay. Those planes already in the air, in order to stay together, were simply circling overhead waiting to launch a coordinated attack.

This used precious fuel they would need to get to the Japanese fleet. More than one pilot reported thinking this would be a one-way mission simply because they wouldn't have enough fuel to return.

Finally, 32 dive bombers were sent off without waiting for the torpedo bombers. They made it to the designated spot, fully expecting to see a large Japanese armada. What they found, though, was an empty ocean. Where was the Kido Butai? The Americans were forced to do a "box" search to find the Japanese before running out of fuel.

Two pilots did indeed have to ditch their fuel-empty planes. But finally, the flight commander spotted a lone ship proceeding at a fast clip, leaving a wake that looked like a white arrow painted on the surface of the sea. This ship pointed the way for our bombers to find the Japanese strike force.

Ten minutes later they found their targets. However, confusion soon erupted. Due to a communication glitch, rather than splitting the valuable targets below, the majority of dive bombers went at the first carrier in sight. Twenty-seven of the planes aimed at the same Japanese aircraft carrier. Well, of course it turned to a smoldering ruin, but that left only three planes to attack another. Two perfect hits on a second aircraft carrier sank the ship immediately, due in no small part to the fully fueled, torpedo-loaded planes on deck and the excellent aim of our pilots.

In five minutes, three quarters of the Japanese mobile force were on their way to the bottom of the ocean, thanks to airstrikes launched from our three carriers. Sadly, our Yorktown was hit yet again and sank a few days later.

A recap of Midway miracles:

- If Seward hadn't made sure Midway was under American authority, we wouldn't have had a base exactly where we needed one about eighty years later.
- Had the attack on Pearl Harbor taken out all three of our aircraft carriers, there's no way we could have defended Midway only months later.

- Had the first squadron waited for their torpedo bombers, surely the rest of the dive bombers would have run out of fuel.
- If that one little Japanese straggler hadn't been late to their attack party, our flyers might never have found the armada before running out of fuel.
- If the Yorktown hadn't been repaired in time, it would have left our side more seriously under-equipped. As it was, Japanese planes were ahead of ours technologically.
- Had the remaining three dive bombers not acted quickly upon the confusion of so many of their own planes attacking the same ship, they might not have succeeded in sinking the second carrier before Japan could retaliate.

The Battle of Midway seriously impacted the Japanese Navy. It was a battle we weren't "supposed" to win—in fact our own leaders didn't think the odds were in our favor since the Kido Butai was renowned for its strength. But our success ended the string of Japanese Navy successes and "turned the tide" (pun intended) in our direction.

It's tragic to celebrate a victory that obviously ended the lives of so many men on both sides. However, having heard first-hand what our then-enemies from the land of the rising sun were doing to our prisoners of war, and would continue to do for the duration of the war, I can't imagine what the world would be like today had we lost.

All I can say about this chapter is: don't inexplicable experiences open the possibility of a spiritual realm? Perhaps God really is involved in what goes on around here, both personally and nationally.

Afterword

If you've read this far, first of all, thank you. Whether you're already a firm believer in Christ, a nominal believer, or not a believer at all, I'm grateful for the time you invested to see why my husband, my brother and I believe what we believe.

I'm old enough to know that sometimes, though, people just cannot agree on things regarding faith. Inevitably we meet someone who disputes whatever we say. This is part of being human—each of us decides on our own, and sometimes for complicated reasons.

J. Warner Wallace has spoken to many atheists since his own adult conversion to faith. He lists four reasons why sometimes it's not about the material and whether it's sound. Something else may stand in the way of taking the time to consider the evidence surrounding the Bible as God's Holy Book.

- Sometimes it's about **politics**. Oh no! I can hear members of my family warning me not to get into this subject. Stick with me, though, because I'm not going too deep into this very thorny topic. I agree with J. Warner that sometimes people may shut down discussion because they have a pre-conceived image of a close-minded, judgmental Christian who represents the opposite of political and social issues they hold dear. My hope here is that somehow both sides can cut each other some slack, because there are many reasons for our dearly held values. I think we must realize it's the Holy Spirit Who is likely the only One able to touch some hearts (not our own tactical argument). Perhaps a person unwilling to consider the God of the Bible because of social issues might want to ask themselves if it could be *perceptions* of what the Bible says, not the evidence itself, standing in the way of faith. God may even support some of your issues.

- Sometimes it's **family history** standing in the way. Perhaps a particularly harsh parent, an earthly father who made a heavenly one seem someone to fear or hate, or a set of rules or traditions so unhealthy it's almost impossible to look at alternative evidence. These kinds of deeply ingrained experiences can seem too big to see around—maybe the first step is seeing such things as the real barrier.
- Sometimes it's less about Christianity's truths than it is about **Christians**. This is where our human sin nature gets in the way, in or outside our flawed family experiences. Perhaps a pastor, elder, or older church member misrepresented the God of the Bible so severely that it's impossible to separate experience from evidence that God is Who He said He is. He is as grieved by being used for evil as any truly loving being would be, only more so because His love is perfect. Sometimes reaction to evidence of God is more emotional than purely rational.
- Finally, some people reject the Bible because they think Christians are dangerously **stupid**. We have "blind faith." Or "faith has killed more people in history than any other force." (Not technically true since pursuit of power is actually the worst culprit, but that's another

topic.) The accusation that Christians are blind to reality is part of the reason I wanted to compile this book. It's important for all Christians to know why we believe what we believe. We should be familiar with the evidence, if only to dispel the incorrect idea that Christians are blind followers fulfilling our innate need to worship something—especially these days, when worshiping ourselves is so in vogue.

And as Hugh Ross says: sometimes it's about **surrendering**. Hugh has spoken to many groups of scientists, presenting complicated evidence that this ancient Book we call Holy really does reveal remarkable insight into science and creation and history and humankind. When asking fellow scientists why they still discount Christianity, many admit it's because they simply don't want to hand over control of their lives to a God who may tell them to stop doing something they don't want to stop doing, or start doing something they don't want to start doing.

It might be a good idea to dig a little deeper into why the idea of faith can be automatically rejected, just as we're challenged to give a rational reason for the faith we hold. Everyone should have reasons to believe what they believe, no matter what they believe.

Finally, people we love or even just meet may accept or reject God. It may come down to the one thing we can do: pray. God is far more effective at touching lives than we are, and sometimes we don't have what we want because we don't ask.

Once again, thank you for reading this, my most personal of books. If I don't get to hang out with you in this lifetime, my deepest desire is to see you in heaven where we'll certainly have the time. I'll meet you there!

Acknowledgments

Special thanks to the pastors and authors from whom I've learned so much:
Mark Gilbert
Skip Heitzig
Jack Hibbs
David Jeremiah
John Lennox
David Limbaugh
Josh McDowell
Stephen Meyer
Hugh Ross
Lee Strobel

Special thanks to historian Mark Peterson for helping me better understand the history of Israel.

My favorite sources for much of the material contained in this book:
A Matter of Days by Hugh Ross
Case for a Creator by Lee Strobel
Cold-Case Christianity by J. Warner Wallace
Creator and the Cosmos by Hugh Ross
I Don't Have Enough Faith to be An Atheist by Norman L. Geisler and Frank Turek
Jesus on Trial by David Limbaugh
Lights in the Sky and Little Green Men by Hugh Ross, Kenneth Samples and Mark Clark

New Evidence That Demands A Verdict by Josh McDowell
What Darwin Didn't Know by Fazale Rana and Hugh Ross
Why The Universe Is The Way It Is by Hugh Ross

Also by Maureen Lang

The Great War Series
Look To The East

Whisper On The Wind

Springtime Of The Spirit

Americans in the First World War
Pieces of Silver

Remember Me

The Cranbury Series
The Cranbury Papermaker

The Cranbury Toymaker

The Cranbury Picturemaker

The Cranbury Troublemaker

The Gilded Legacy
Bees In The Butterfly Garden

All In Good Time

The Matchmaker's Match

Contemporary/Victorian Split Era Series
The Oak Leaves

On Sparrow Hill

Contemporary
My Sister Dilly

About the Author

Maureen Lang writes stories of faith, romance and history. *There Must Be A Reason* is her first full-length work of non-fiction.

Visit her website at:
 www.maureenlang.com

You can contact Maureen at her email address:
 maureen@maureenlang.com

Or via snail mail at:
 591 Press
 PO Box 23
 Belvidere, IL 61008

Notes on Why You Believe

Here's a little room for you to jot down thoughts about your own beliefs or messages you may want to pass on to others as you share this book:

_____

_____

_____

_____

_____

_____

_____

_____

Made in the USA
Columbia, SC
30 May 2025